at the
Ocean's Verge

BOOKS BY RALPH GUSTAFSON

Poetry

The Golden Chalice (1935)
Epithalamium in Time of War (1941)
Lyrics Unromantic (1942)
Flight into Darkness (1944)
Rivers Among Rocks (1960)
Rocky Mountain Poems (1960)
Sift in an Hourglass (1966)
Ixion's Wheel (1969)
Selected Poems (1972)
Theme and Variations for Sounding Brass (1972)
Fire on Stone (1974)
Corners in the Glass (1977)
Soviet Poems (1978)
Sequences (1979)
Landscape with Rain (1980)
Conflicts of Spring (1981)
Gradations of Grandeur (1982)
Manipulations on Greek Themes (1983)
The Moment Is All (1983)

Drama

Alfred the Great (1937)

Short Stories

The Brazen Tower (1974)
The Vivid Air (1980)

Anthologies (As Editor)

Pelican Anthology of Canadian Poetry (1942)
A Little Anthology of Canadian Poets (1943)
Canadian Accent (1944)
The Penguin Book of Canadian Verse (1958, 1967, 1975)
   (new edition in preparation)

Ralph Gustafson

at the Ocean's Verge

SELECTED POEMS

BLACK SWAN BOOKS

*The poems included in this volume have been selected by the book's
editor, John Walsh, and represent necessarily a partial and partisan
view of the wide range of Ralph Gustafson's poetry.*

Acknowledgment: material for the *Introduction* of this book has been
excerpted from "The Saving Grace," *Canadian Literature*, no. 97
(Summer 1983) and from "The Sequence," published in *Sequences* (Windsor: Black Moss Press, 1978).

to Betty from Philadelphia

First edition

Published by

BLACK SWAN BOOKS Ltd.
P. O. Box 327
Redding Ridge, CT 06876

ISBN 0-933806-16-7

Contents

III Overtones

IV Fire on Stone

V   In Dispraise of Great Happenings

VI   Aesthetics at Delphi

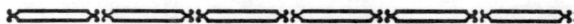

VII Armorial

VIII Poems on Themselves and Music

IX Coda

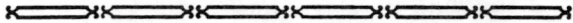

Preface

Rᴀʟᴘʜ Gᴜꜱᴛᴀꜰꜱᴏɴ is that rarity amongst contemporary North American writers: a poet of articulate eloquence. The language of his poems is concentrate; fulfilling Ezra Pound's dictum, the poems are charged with intensity—exploding in the mind and heart sumultaneously. They are flares which illuminate both the external and interior landscape, clarifying the obscure tracks of thought and emotion—as well as being trajectories of assertion. They cut through vagaries and ambiguities to make *statements;* condensing and defining experience, they dare to venture personal utterance.

Gustafson is sharply alert to the sound of words, to the poem's *melos.* And, indeed, Gustafson is a poet deeply involved with music as both theme and technique. Lines of poems reverberate, resonating with the warmth and clarity of a bow passing over the strings of a cello. The mind is keened thereby; their very sonority evoking response.

Gustafson's poetry is humanist: it explores human existence, from the concrete depths to the open and uncertain heights. Pain and ecstasy are interwoven in the fabric of these poems; bitterness, humor, irony and sensual joy are not alien to them, nor are the "complex simplicity" of sense experience and the humble fact of love. Rooted in *eros,* Gustafson's vision extends outward, octopus-like, to grapple with the world. As Confucius put it: first, order in oneself; then outward order follows. Yet the unheeding spike of history resists. Personal intimacy is contrasted with the agony of historical existence. Both are enmeshed; the encounter, inevitable. Another's pain injures the body of humanity. Yet despair does not blunt; rather it sharpens perception. Irony, contradiction, disparity edges vision. Sublimity abides, even in the midst of absurdity. Love is the pivot. Such is the contention of these poems.

Collected in this edition are poems drawn from the entirety of Gustafson's writings—extending over some 49 years (1935–83) and 20 volumes of poetry. While at times the locale is Canada, the voice is international—the experience of human existence being universal. The seasons, the skies, the lands are specific; the perceptions are shared. When writing about a province, Gustafson avoids the pitfall of provincialism. Rather the references range through time and space, encompassing ancient Egypt, classical Greece, Renaissance Italy, 19th century Europe, as well as the chaos of the modern world.

The dialogue engaged in is symphonic; both polyphonic and vital. Specific figures, places, artifacts have become emblematic. In these poems, the facts of both past and present—a fragment of Egyptian stone; a Greek potsherd; light caught in cut crystal; color spilled by stained-glass upon stone; a carved rifle-butt—form a living archaeology, separate voices set against the dissonance of a machine gun's snap, the cry of a child in pain, or the blast of a bomb, shattering the landscape's silence. Ground bass and lyric melody alternate in these poems—or rather form a chord, the sound of the vertical strata of human existence; the *vox humana.*

John Walsh

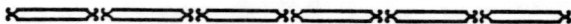

Introduction

THE SAVING GRACE IS POETRY. If one defines poetry as the enlightenment of fact, the worth of experience, the attainment of sensibility, the establishment of compassion—in any of the ways in contradiction to the disharmony, the structural collapse, the pollution of right ritual, the violence and disgrace of our times— then poetry is the saving grace. It is so because it exhibits the worth of sensible harmony, of man with man, of man with himself, of man with nature. We need this worth if we are to survive even on the most pragmatic level. And poetry does not leave man there; its procedure is never toward the lowest common denominator, but rather the highest factor; it is elitist, it demands the ablest men, the rarest quotient; it is after the elimination of the mediocre; it desires to be left with only the most peaceable delight, sensual and cerebral. With a fraction of this desirable attainment achieved, our world is solvent and worthful.

Poetry fools no one with romanticism and sentimentality. Its commencement is from the crudest foundation of disillusionment, the wringingest awareness of irony, the very hatred and futility that is in historical mankind. Poetry is restless from the absurdity of not knowing; the refusal of the heavens to answer is its subject-matter. There they are, those black holes stuck in heaven.

LOOKING AROUND ITSELF, poetry is aware of not much to praise. Wallace Stevens's attributive to poetry, "A sacrament of praise," diminishes itself. The majesty of man is derided. Youth is crucified in Cambodia for stealing a handful of rice; the bomb is hurled indifferently, a leg comically flies across the restaurant; in County Sligo a child is blown up in the boat of his grandfather; a little girl runs screaming down a road in Vietnam trying to tear the flaming napalm off her; a smell comes from ovens; treads roll in the streets of Budapest, Prague, Warsaw; accident is denied admission at a hospital. What newer? The poet makes his poem out of the unstructured world; he is driven to the last expression; he finds his lines in grievousness; his rhythm halts. His thoughts are confined to narrow nights.

So when the world seems insoluble, he falters. Lacklustre, he gathers in to coteries. He goes to green gardens and cultivates his own shade against the glaring sun. He cuts up useful words into jots and syllables, scatters empty spaces around. He praises silence. He draws pictures with his typewriter. But the game does not satisfy. No one listens. Solipsism won't do. He gets sick of his ego, gets bored with pretension. There is nothing for it but negative capability, losing himself to find himself. The true world greets him.

He is pitched headlong into irony and clarity. He is made human. The truth is delight. He is moral.

His defence against grievousness is the justification of his profession. Hollow pretension is exposed. He is returned to delight, the first function of his art. He knows that if his poem lies it is a bad poem. A poem cannot lie; its delight is spoiled—the magnificence of structuring verbal music, of moving it through its form so that the very outward existence of itself is the equivalence of its inner conviction, so that the very conveyance is the meaning of what it conveys. Untruth unravels it. He is on the side of love. In agony he faces the world.

A POEM RESIDES IN ITS VERBAL CRAFT and of all the constructions which a poem may take, the sequence, the poem by sections, is the one, I think, most peculiarly contemporary. The architecture accommodates the modern temper. Its structure and complex of meditation, irony and extension, convey the contemporary world of incompletion and, at the same time (in accordance with Poe's injunction), maintain tension. It accommodates our imperative for lyricism, resolution (in the musical sense), comprehensible ambition, and, to the extent of these successes, supplies

coherence if not inclusive unity. A further demand by this age of romantic survival is met: the structure satisfies the personal desire to shape heterogeneous experience, sublimates the need of quotidian accomplishment; it can, if it wills, serve as a chronological poetic journal, the momentum of which approaches the conceptual and physical continuity of the narrative. The sequence provides worthwhile evidence of the progress of a soul. The world is in enough fragments.

A poem is superior to the extent that the verbal music heard is the meaning; otherwise, it is prose. As an art, music has the superiority over poetry in that thought in music is sensuous. Poetry without thought is vapid. Its struggle therefore is not to become prose. In its greatest reaches it achieves the condition of music. But whatever the degree, the poem to be a poem must be rightly heard and rhythmically felt. The poet can be as nonverbally tone-deaf as Yeats was, but his ear must hear, his pulse must respond.

The sequence is close to the construction of music; at best, it achieves a nearness, almost an identity, with music. The shaping of the turmoil of contemporary experience can best be achieved by the procedures of music through which the sequence moves: the progression of exposition, development and resolution: the sonata, not only in its meaning of *suonare,* to sound, but in its transformation of suite into symphony. Movement is made through a modulation of keys in affinity, into the "home" key; from cruel April to *shantih,* if you will, from consultation with the dead to the "men not destroyers" who end Pound's *Cantos.* The movement, at last, being toward dominant significance. The poem structured in this way has marked our century: Eliot composing his four quartets, Stevens playing his blue guitar, Crane as Orpheus building his bridge, Pound confounding chaos with sequential counterpoint.

Ralph Gustafson

I At the Ocean's Verge

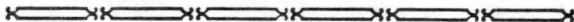

Prolegomenon at Midnight

It is the rusted moon moves foamless parting sky,
Her salty starboard stowed still with beauty.
She weighed westerly soon.

A figure merely. But it was once, I mused,
Granted to swashbuckle tide and seed and star
On schedule, scoff departures.

Youth is not sharp enough. The oak in the woods
Accurate as irony, he saw her off,
The chance deliberate,

Blustered his blossomy April of gangplank failures
Whose weather's welter was a mathematics,
Winter's punctual plot.

Thwarted by swagger and love's lavish, what
Do we remember of the thousandth rose
Or copulation's squander?

What only solver but that daredown doter
Launched like a lackluck whose heroics, none
Of our laurel, target love?

Oh, nothing now but I must out of oceans
Lift leviathan like a Job, my Moby
Dangle on a hook.

That is to say, nothing's left to do
But drag up god in the wig of my words. The rest's
A muddle of farewells.

At the Ocean's Verge

I SHOULD PRAY but my soul is stopt.
This is a bombast world: fig-trees,
Snow, macacos, ocean's hurl
And surf and surge, on applebough
As crag whose cave holds kraken or
With comb of coral mermaid cuddles.
All's mad majesty and squander,
And x and y or zodiac
Excreting wizard mathematics
Like a slew of ebbtide worms
Won't solve it. The sand is miles and packt
And moonlights wash the gnawings of
A million years. The globe cants so,
It's miracle a man can walk it.
Listen to him: *I'll say my prayers*
And set mine eyes on kingdom come.
I'll jump the prickly hedge and scratch
Them in again. I'll. I'll.
Not Hesperides, I warrant,
No matter what you will. Try.
Scour this heaven-hung kettle of fish—
The sweep has greater satisfaction
Up a chimney cleaning soot
With good soap after. Oh, you'll hoist
And heft your stature by a hair—
No one but the Barber wiser.
    Hear how this ocean thurls and thunders!
    Crashing foams and ravels once
    Was muted marble Athens owned.

On This Sea-Floor

THE EVENING FALLS. The sunset burns
The edge of grass. Where the beach fence
Climbs down, the curlews are done with history.
Sea-tide

On the rocks lifts kelp and is fecund.
The shaped oyster sucks himself in
In sand and the razor-clam zips and is floorless vertical.
Into the ocean

The crab crawls, dragging an entrail.
On this sea-floor there is no disparity.
Conches blown by sea-boys are filled with stomach.
Delicacies void.

Acceptances inhere. Haphazard
The efficient Laughter's driven home.
In salty caverns rests the perfect squid.
Men die.

Shoreward fish affirm the sense
Of humour. On the beach at Viareggio,
Byron turned and was sick, Shelley failing
To burn on the pyre,

The guts salt-soaked—a reasonable
Wetness, yet the legend how
These tidal waters roll upon the world,
A claptrap work.

Oedipus innocent wipes his jelly
Eyes; Job recounts his boils.
Limbless birth exemplifies the banter.
Byron, rather,

Threw up. We use an only insolence,
That gropings should extend to men
And glories wash the steady stars; capsize
      Constant God,

Wrapping up our ocean elegies
In thunderous jests, turning deaf ears
To the hobnob silence of the empty shores;
      Try our luck—

Dragging up Jonah with our whale
And fizzling Icarus with our wits.
Hamlet plays his ghost at Elsinore.
      The catch is considerable:

Caesar goes; Alexander
Catches cold. Beethoven rages.
From the Parthenon, the Venetian lowers Athena's
   chariot,
      Brings down the house.

The thunder's slim—not loud enough
To gag hilarious heaven. . . . We have
A like compassion. Lear in his rain, crying
      O, O,

And age on the pavement of 14th Street. . . .
The soft-haired prawn is ensconced in his kingdom.
Stars congregate and mark the runnings of
      The ebbing tide. . . .

The lighthouse catches the mermaids' bums.
Shells hold sea-thunder.
On the sands, his trident weedy and crown awry,
      Old Proteus naps.

Rondo in Triads

1

History marks the lines on
The palm of my hand the way
I go.

2

The long slender bone with
The manacle on it is my
Right arm.

3

And in my eyes is the sight
Of the soft bruise from
The gunbutt.

4

I sit in my chair and the arch
Of my ankle is split
By the spike.

5

I watch the man running with his child
From the bomb. I intend to go out to help
Them.

6

I mistake the stars of heaven
As I choose between my right hand
And my other.

7

Whole cities abuse God for
The manner of their choice. Persia
And Rome.

8

Scarlatti, famous for crossing hands,
Became so fat he was unable to play
In this position.

9

O I could cry out with beauty
Of hills, the poem's hardness that is
My sex.

10

"The sex member has a poetic power
Like a meteor," says Miro. I looked
At the heavens.

11

"The simplest things give me ideas," he says,
Walking across his unmarked canvas
In dirty shoes.

12

The slanted plaster ceiling of the attic
Had cracks in it Michelangelo
Made use of.

13

The keyboard, recall, got that width
Because ladies in hoopskirts loved
To play duets.

14

They say Mozart crossed the Alps
Without once looking up from the scores
On his lap.

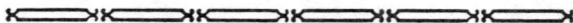

15

Cézanne's apples. Who cares whether
They are sweet or sour? I love
Appleness.

16

An investigating spectroscope
Declares flowers are naturally blind
To green.

17

Fap. I listen to beavers. *Fap.*
Hunt a bird who has to learn
To build a nest.

18

I walk with my love in the wide world.
Comets burst and pincers close
Around a moth.

19

And the earth is indifferent to the diamond in it.
"Oh, mes amis, j'ai nostalgie de la boue!"
Cried Rachel.

20

Along my coatsleeve the fire
Of thought. In my mouth the taste
Of words.

The Remarkable Heavens

WE ARE ALL sailing in a circle,
The globe leans towards the seasons.
We are a part of heavenly declensions
Doing what we have to do, ice
And icy icebergs north, or, inclined
The other way, steamy swamps,
The damp crocodile in them,
O tears. What shall we do
Taken for a ride around the sky?
Stars blink in the passage, the sun
Goes up and down while the hermit prays.
Yesterday we passed through Leo,
The zodiac a ninth month gone and
No parturition. Last
Monday fortnight I observed
The moon at the lake-edge with my love.
It was only half there. Tomorrow
I master astronomy and play like Liszt.
I can remember sirens I cranked
Going round corners, fires dreamed;
Cabooses rode. Now I take up
Heaven. Orion went out just now
Quenched by a horizon and the pole star
Just swung around and stayed there.

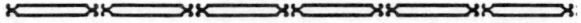

Bestiary

AT THE TROUGH and then the urinal,
A mighty magnificence is mankind.
Nature has us stumped. Spirit's soiled.
Listen to him rant then consider
These two colts in fettle, they push
Not, neither do they pretend.
Or ponder this baboon, it does not
Laugh too loudly at its own jokes
Nor go to Helsinki to give away
Patrimony, it is tolerant of whether God
Is coconut or banana,
It is a very Christian soul,
Not feeling virtuous through hate.
The cat, sleek, washes itself.
It is a dignified domain. Ducks
Stand naturally on their heads, swans
Are silent and dying, the elephant
Seeks privacy, does not trumpet
Imperfection and go to the moon.
Pre-eminently the spider is openly subtle.
Even Death
Seeks various considerate ways to make
His ever appealing presence known.

Circus

Hung by wire. Four and four
(*The figure Jung said expressed*
The ultimate divine reality within us)
The figures of the four girls,
The four guys, spangled,
Walking the tightrope,
Flaw each side of them across
The tent top, birth to death,
Equilibrist, each toe delicate
Set in front, Natasha upside down
On Vasily's head. Strobe
Lights play, drum
Points, the whole Copernicus put
On a step . . . . She's pretty. He,
Axiom. They reach the platform,
Whirl, salute the world.
Next time, next time:
Misunderstanding,
Slackened love . . . .

The Certainty of Triumph

SPRING MOVES and pallid under the leaves
The prophecy of winter. The thrust of pure
Rhythms urgent undoes the long year
And the sorrows and the snow and this late
                          knowledge of death.
The wedge of iris breaks earth.

Sits a stone, he, weighted down with dreams,
Hears rhythms possible, grass and thighs, thinks
Green attainments into being, crosstree,
Resurrection, cockfriction. Fool!
Dots his *i* with diamond.

II Conflicts of Spring

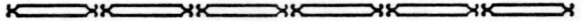

Biography

WHAT TIME the wily robin tuggeth worm,
Dragging my grandsire from reluctant dust,
Did I, through fatal lips of unction thrust,
Lunge headmost lidded from Cassandra's womb:
Puberal, still with bended bow did shoot
Heroic arrows tipped at the fabulous sky,
Whose silver barbed the snow. To testify
The cryptic acorn plus the accurate root,
I, fool, with words of paper, scissors, paste,
Mailed awkward anagrams to Love and Death,
And lagged and loosed the ravelling threads that baste
This bone to cerements of flesh. Beneath
The purchase of my present jaw, I taste
The apple twixt the tombstones of my teeth.

The Birds South

ALL THE NESTS of the songbirds were seen,
The boughs bare. They hung desolate,
The birds south. Between the boughs,
The sky silver, the sky blue above,
The sun near setting and the work
Nearly done, the dirt by the stone wall,
Pushed against it when they fixed
The road, now spread evenly so all
Is just, when snow melts and thaw
Runs down the slopes hazardously freezing,
The temperature down; the shovel, put
Away.
       The years pass. Once the strip
By the wall was lawn, green and held
By seed the squirrels love against
Their winter, time other than now.
Memory caught my breath.
                Nothing
Had changed visibly, the lake the same,
Water does not change, just
The shore lines as the seasons will,
The sky silver, as usual near winter, and the nests,
Hidden all summer long, now there
For the eye to find, source of that
Green madness when in the ear is song
And adulations of foliage praise
Renewals and scorn existence,
                    now
Green unseen, the birds south.

Landscape with Rain

I LOOKED at the landscape quickly as though
I had not deserved it. Too much time
Had passed and I had not observed
The flash of colour that the leaves show
As rain falls turning the under
Sides to silver with the weight.
The hills move with translucence.
I was careless how the heart revives,
The sight of a horse standing and how
As the moon goes through the night the resonance
Of silence is without birds or any
Hindrance to completion. Light astonishes
The mind with new wonder at dawn.
       These things are felt with guilt
As the days pass and nothing of them
Has been seen except the concern
Of their going.
          I now walk with suspense,
The going not less real but stopping
An uneven of times with astonishment, getting
Where I have to with adequate concern,
Time shortens very quickly,
But seeing at least how the moss
Is green in patches under the rain
Where the boulder stands exposed and the lake
Is come on grandly swept.

Ramble on What's Gone Before

I FLINCH AGAIN, knowing it, death. I'm against it.
I am used to myself, skin, flooding crimson
Peeled, smelled musk, touching and taste,
That elusive variegated vinegar and berry.
Bury! *Howya* . . . Who would be without
His own intimacies, coign and groin, earnestness
And what else? My god—the poignancy of music,
Of that . . . And daybreak which at the peroration
Throws in its instant the doomsday of thought.
The catacombs knew and held onto the cross, and I,
Crossed, hounded by other hanging, the cockwatch,
The one on all men's mind. What a brief hanging
Have we and Petered overwith at what coming!
Sensation solves it only. What shall I love?
Anyone. The chance is short. Brief the savouriest
Body and body of belief. Bawdy, rather.
How to devolve into something like sensational dawn
Not deadly.
           I am for it.

                    All men

Were for it.

              That makes it no easier.

Flux, asserts dual Heraclitus.

                   He
Can have it. Door-slam and stability, that's
What's wanted, hardest ice lasts no more than
A drip, a joy, as all things don't, carved
Marble looked at, her, heard music,
Transit from one room to another room
To what we keep. All things have their last,
Shoes, yardarm, entrances, given shortly,
Shortly take back their permanence.
                 I suppose so.

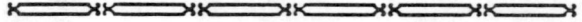

Conflicts of Spring

AFTER THE AUTUMN burns down again
The earth will turn cold until
Spring's opulence. The defection of summer
Is assured and the turning of autumn
Is assured. Burdened with frozen branches
Who will believe in spring's beginning?
It is hard, it is a hard act to follow,
These terminations of blossoms.
Even if the time come of affirmation
It is for others, never permanent
In the slipshod heart;
That will stop.
Trees are green for us only for a time
No matter how they go on
For whatever proclamations of indifference,
Hullaballoo.
The phony clown gets it
However he beats his drum.
Love falls out of love, spring,
A subject in the academies.

The Colour of the Crystal Day

BURNISHED SILVER is the colour of
The still calm winter day.
Spread snow from last night
Lies along the fir branches
Dark beaten green in survival.
The fall was light, only a token
Whiteness of what has gone before
But no less beautiful in crystal freezings
That last a moment held in air,
Symmetry extricable on dark sleeves
Held out. And sorrows still the same:
The man of speech holding out
In amazement his son starved;
Nearer home, she who died
Yesterday. Elegies are constant—
Burnished silver or not, the sky
Of winter. The unanswerable moment
Comes, love denied or had,
This love a condition of being here
As this day still calm, no turmoil
Except what's been or is to be:
The winter crystal and silver light,
The unaccounted-for denial of love.

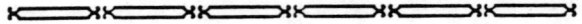

Take, For Instance, Architecture

THERE ARE barrel vaults and groin vaults
And underpitch and quadripartite
Vaults and tierceron and fan,
Counterpoints of cathedral magnificence.
Who will live long enough to distinguish
Coverings, intrados, closures of soaring
Stone, that, from a mortal plot?
I have seen lidded tombs in a row—
At Alys-camps? Certainly nearby.
Glass stained in the sun, on pillar,
Thrown in flame, fire at our feet.
Fire on stone, that hour at Chartres.
Cribs and mouldings. At Cordoba, arches,
All that remains. There is no time.
How shall we distinguish, that rage?
The veriest dawn when we more than awaken
To the intensest moment we finally fear?

Hyacinths with Brevity

You WILL USE whatever watering can
You can, what knife to plant the bulbs.
I smell leaves and crab-apples
On the ground; the crabbed progression is under
Way, blossom poured, jelly
In jars crimson in the sun along
The sill. That hardens it, you tell me.
I shall have toast in the morning.
       But be quick.
The valves of the heart are pesky things
And shut down. We shall no more see
The like of these leaves again. They blow
Across the garden with this brief wind
That blows. So you will use what you can.
This trowel with last summer's caked
Dirt on the blade, and this can
And these forty bulbs which should be
Already in the ground so swift the wind
Blows and brief the constituency
Of sun. This piece of hose will do . . .
But you have the watering can. . . .

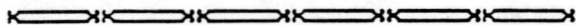

A Gentle Rain Persists

A RAIN PERSISTS and good men die.
Light goes, the dusk comes on.

Even to those who persist with music
Mortality invites itself, Schubert,
Haydn, one with wit his wig
Askew, Schubert coaxed, hoodwinked
By love. Histories spill over
With deductions, yet great men offer
Lives, and all the while, on wharves,
Profitable oranges, permanent lengths
Of pipe, sacks leaned over.

The rain persists. Drops on the glass
Refract the light, red in movement,
Green: the impulse of music . . .

April

THE TILTING OF THE EARTH continuing
Flowers will come up, the sun
Has been out now for nine hours.
New movements following runnels
Down slants between pebbles
Can be remarked by their sparkle;
Motion of air makes puddles
Known. Pale shoots all
Month out of the sun are ready;
The heart aches with the shortness of life.
Patches of soil appear and the lid
Of the bin lies off from the trash
Collector. The end of the violence of the world
Is awaited. Nations hold back.
Young men want their love enfolded;
Fern fronds are furled tight.
Watchers acknowledge the worth of worship.

April, Again

COME ON NOW, I told myself,
Consider wholly love, love
While the sun, after days,
Is out and there is a little joy
In the world between harsh sorrow.
There, again, the sun is out.
Snow spreads aside and April
Is under foot. It is the time,
The time eyes know that grass
Comes under north slopes
And the world is wide on condition
The people in it are widely
Overlooked and what they do
And the heart is willing to concede
Something is about to happen
Like the complicated simplicity
Of blossom and the movement of wings.
Day is able to include even her,
Her movements and practicalities and loving.
Death hasn't yet stepped in.
It's joy, partly, and the heart is voluble
In the way first mentioned above.
On the earth sun is come.

Morning's Light

Even the suffering's worth it.
When the ground-phlox blooms
What of the pain; there is cessation;
The jonquil is white, the oriole
Sings? No? Then surely there is
Remembrance, that first ecstasy?
Music dwells in the soul.
Perhaps that first hearing of Sibelius'
Tuonela, or even at dawn
Something as simple as that oriole,
Liquid, crazy with love heard
In the far garden, the elm by the lake's
Side, intuitive with lopsided possession
And morning and sun and love.

There is a sobering beyond all
Comprehension. It is this leaving
Of suffering, of birds, oriole and elm
And remembrance and lake's side,
And hearing of music.

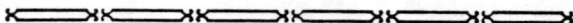

Of Green Steps and Laundry

THE MAN will put a large-headed nail,
Shiny as silver, into the green step,
Straightening winter's bias and spring
Thaw and his hammer will knock it crooked,
The bird come obtrusively to the bough above,
And it will have to be done again, and that
Will be important; and she will hang
Blue and white shirts and a patched quilt
On the laundry line that runs from the kitchen
Step to the yard telephone pole and sheets
That smell of winter's cold, and the pulley
Each time the line is launched will squeak,
And that will be important; and neither
She nor the man pounding the clear air
Fixing the green step with another nail,
Will be aware of the importance, twenty
Years later thought of by him
Who drove nails and saw laundry,
Who thought little of cardinals and clothespins
And now loves life, loves life.

The Woods, Still Winter

THE SNOW in the far woods falling, he bends
Down to remove the snow from his mukluks,
Looking around him gazing at the falling
Snow, wondering at the continual fall,
Thinking of the fire burning, the place
He loves over all places but loving
The clearing, the white birch (*again*)
Slanting the firs heavy with fresh
Burden, the continual snow falling.
He thinks of the impossibility perhaps
Of coming tomorrow. The woods need
The man in it somewhere; concern.
With his finger he takes the white rim
Of snow away from his boots, looks up
At the winter a moment; moves on.

Snow Lay along the Long Bough

SNOW LAY along the long bough
As if that could scare birds,
As if constancy were done for. But I doubted
That could scare denizens: I have seen
Sparrows scrabbling, a squirrel indifferent,
In the arms of drifts; conversely,
Day brought up short in summer's
Term and an hour later, sky
That was rubbed silver dazzling
The eye, struck across dark
Winter. The mind knows that music
Will never stop. The constancy is,
Who will hear it? Sadness lies
Beneath all music. Four seasons
Are not enough. The heart, paced,
Halts, birds sing and die in time
Not knowing it. But there's the dignity!
The mind's apart. Seeing creation
Cease, we stand on eminences knowing it,
Look back on brevities, ahead to lost
Fortunes, so that we know renewals. A crux
Not got out of. Except these lungs stop.
Yes, I have seen men eased out indifferently,
Birds stupid on winter boughs.

A Night of Thick Snow and Then Sun

THE SUN broke out of the dark of winter
And there was a dust of snow in the air—
"Dark" not quite the right word,
Thick wet snow had fallen throughout the night
And the narrowest twig of every tree
Had a line of white—how each held so much
I would not know—there was a crosshatch
To the world—so "dark" was not
The right word—the word of the Lord
Would have been better—never mind—
The slightest stir of air brought down
Falls of it and the sun against
All that world of crossings came out.
My breath caught.
There was an exaltation—
Suffering was everywhere
But if you felt any sort of opposite
There was that reaction.
Failed of wholeness we pursue nothing,
Chemistry; the slightest giving,
Love perhaps knows itself
And anger comes.

　　　　　　　The sun came out.
The night had been oppressive,
Without purpose. The air filled
With dust of fallen snow.
According to admission my heart beat,
My breath held, and I
Was against anything but being alive.

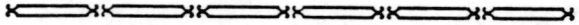

Praise of Margins

And of the white moon (be praised, O Lord)
—SAINT FRANCIS OF ASSISI

THE EGRET debugs the cows in Grenada,
The white egret perambulating
His dinner as *naucrates ductor* does
His shark. Ocean teems; on land
The tanager wings a million lice.
All is one to Brother Francis.
Love's the pivot; otherwise
Is scales and hair. By that, least
Is most, this worn and dusty challenge
Thereby mock of sequestration
Nor the forfeit for redemption.
Praise to the weevil who lives on seeds,
Whose nosy head's prolonged to snout;
To the sidling crab compliment.
All is news of God; sequestered
Moon, exaltation. Laud
To the burdened yak who has no need
To shorten breath on mountains, the padded
Cat. Daystream magnify.
God's His least thing, not
To be given up to be got to. Dusky
Day awakes with praise, threadbare
Worms rejoice at starry night.

A Slight Wind and White Flowers

THE SLIGHTEST WIND moved the white wave
Of saxifrage—the five-petal flower
That tumbles stone walls, destruction that likes
Spring. A bee clung and swung a stem of it,
The wind not the only mover, teeming
Propagation was also,
Thigh-carried pollen. The sequence
Only needed death in it
To complete all topics possible
To be thought of. But death wasn't
In it this time, the afternoon
Was too forgetful, sun on rockfoil,
The bee at work, termination something
That could take care of itself. Small
Wars were on elsewhere but here were acts
Without man in them—except that someone
Has to be around to make the act of perceiving.
Luck had it that ambition wasn't around,
Only life teeming and a day for it,
Not to die in but to accomplish
Divine events, acrobatics on stems,
A slight wind and white flowers.

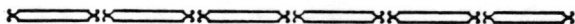

Cadenza with Green Sail

W<small>HY</small>, then, this world is brought to great conclusions.
The extensions of this factual night are beauty,
The way the mind sees the mud and stones.

Not the humid day, the dark in the cellar
Where old music records that whirled, warp,
Where the invisible rust has a going at it,

Not these are the reality, not in themselves,
Not the bare statement is satisfactory
To what we demand that is more than what it exists in,

What's beyond stark-staring is the meaning:
Not the fiery mist in Orion's sword
But the coming suns, not the star but its nightly

Reflection in the lake, nor the lake's *stasis*
But the walk beside it. Not her cheek, her shoulder,
Also what I love—or you your own substitution.

Any example will do: the moisture drawn down
In a majesty of moon and icicle that winter;
This morning, the blue-sails down the lake,

The green or blue depending on how the refraction
Of light meets the eye. Who hoisted
Green and what do we make of it? I had grave

Wonders standing beside recumbent Buddha;
El Greco was knocked out of my head.
So you look at these stars and think wondrous

Extensions, such as eternal comprehension
Of space and star, coincidence constructing
Time—the whole panoply done for the sake of

Silver, a tension of silver over mud,
Stones; my love; the irrevocability by which
A thing is; great propagations!

And so, in the relation of yardstick and yardstick,
Where I mediate the world is a green sail.
I get through it by dint of honesty.

III   Overtures

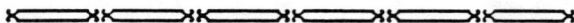

Halfway through March

THIS IS THE TIME of seeds,
For the edges of red shoots
Under leaves, for open
Snowdrops though. Evidence of spring.
Patches of snow hold out
On the banks lying north
Where the drift was thickest.
The curling rink
Holds a sugaring off.

The bed is made
With the fresh sheets,
The window is open,
The double one pushed back
On its crooked side brackets.
The noise of the rush of meltwater
Pours down the steep roadway
Where it shouldn't run,
The culvert still frozen solid.

I try to adjust what is known
To new announcements.
The rage isn't easy.
Small minds persuade their triumph,
The electrode harms
Where no mark is left,
Abraham puts the knife
Through the throat of Isaac.
Channels run littleness.

Overtones

1

THE WIND is indifferent.
Moving through far trees,
It moves. Whether we live
Or die. Near gardens
The scent of flowers
Gathers the air,
Encloses intimacies.
Do not be mistaken.
Corners are got around,
Stillness precedes comings,
The wind is seen only
Because of bent leaves.
Two trees grind together.
Bird song
Makes no difference,
Train binoculars,
Warm summer
Gives before the wind.

Of all the heavens
This is our derivation.
The successful stars shine.
The foliage never still.

2

The clouds move across the sky
Pushed by the wind. In the afternoon
Half-light they lend a radiance
Where the sun comes through and the edges of cloud
Are glory. In the east, at Munich the newly dead
Are scattered at the *Oktoberfest*.

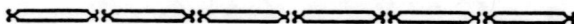

A midge bloated with blood
Runs crazy over the arm
Of the garden chair as I watch.

3

The flake was too hard for a mood of loving
Or remembering. Intricate crystal,
The fall was hard in lines oblique
One way with the wind, across
The air, the road, the fence-rails.
One walked against it. The world was bitter.
Figure-skating went on; zealots
Leaned on unique rifles longing
For understanding. The sharp snow
Fell continually; made footmarks
Were obliterated in an hour.

Noonhour

THERE IS A HUMMING along the wires.
It is not the passenger plane in the heavens
Heavy with purpose nor the hot flies
Near at hand in the grassy air.

It is not even along the wires.
I thought it was. Hot summer produces
Such illusions, alfalfa heavyheaded
Going down to the edge of the cool river.

The humming is an intolerable sound . . .
The nerves stretch. It must stop.
They are making, manufacturing something
At noon. The end of the beginning.

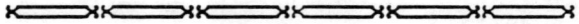

Afternoon

THE JET bores the blue. Drives in.
The military are practising security,
Training summer. There's a chill in the air.
Every once in a while a narrow breeze
Comes in, just a gentle sideswipe,
Over the hedge and then past the lone aster.
The hummingbird has gone south.
Though there is a blue sail on the lake,
A blue candystick canvas
Going this way and then that
Catching the chill breeze,
Though not all summer employment
Has gone,
The plane is up there seeking assurance,
A civilized man and his grandson
Have just been blown up in their boat
In the grand scene of Sligo,
The Irish love violence.
A terrible beauty is born.
      Why that aster in the garden
Should be a lone aster,
Why not more of them
Royal in a row,
Is not immediately apparent,
Someone away for the earlier months perhaps
Who owned the garden.
Asters are annuals.
When the sun went in
In that loud heaven,
Summer intimations,
Civilities, were over.

In a Time of Minor Wars

THIS green tree
with May now,
this lilac
goes breaking with more
sun,
under the soil are crowded
waters.
Great moments urge
galaxies.
Of lake and grass
prodigious repetitions,
alterations,
happen.

Children know not
this is ordered.
Against the children we have laid
interdictions,
virtues,
in a certain light the body is
        not to be enjoyed,
the lilac unnatural.

Gothic Fugue

THE WORLD's ill-handled sorrows intervene
And all the ornaments of clouds and trees
And water-broken sun denounce their joy
Rococo to the grief. Far from this hide-out
Hung with summer, leaves, the climbing vine,
Tomorrows crumble like a rhetoric
The hungry stare at.

Across the garden roses flaunt their sex,
The heavy orchards generation spill
As though the world has room for natural love.
As well expect Belshazzar's peacock fanning
Beettops with the parlance of his tail.
Against the hayrick Onan clockwise plucks
The petals off:

He isn't: God is love. What difference—
The method's no more yokel than x and y,
The amorous mathematics come out odd
And, at the pitch of almost, 's interruption.
God is lately turned a physicist
And got himself within parentheses.
The sunset goes.

Now in the evening of the rounding world
The drafty churchbell tolls the faithful in:
Lilies toil not, neither do they spin;
The raven's clothed. But there are doubts, the best
Advice declares the lilies have too grave
A scent and, like the smoky poppy, please,
To bribe the brain

With Easter; morticians swear the raven's never
Met but men will rave and swear they smell
Friday's mortal meaning. The orchards fade.

Among these northern vegetables, darkness falls,
The whippoorwill proves his notes and all the heaven's
Starry sky—configurations grounded
In a cabbage.

Fumbling fear, O certain generation
Damnably shoved on, owning love, that shoulders
All this galaxy and garb, nothing
More is left who, patching solipsisms
Up with safety-pins, in conclave sits
To say who owns the vacuum. Nothing does.
Midnight thickens.

The garden multiplies with careful growths:
Concatenations propagate themselves
And like a logic hitch the ground; agamic
Fungus, torts, digested truths, attach
Their stuff for mouths to munch on. Eyeballs
Hear the confidential reasoning.
Children shriek.

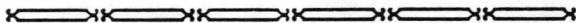

Basque Lover

IN THE MOUNTAIN-FASTNESS lies
Nearer flesh than husbandries,
Fatal lover lipping mud
Pliant to his amorous mood.

On Cabuerniga's hill
Lavish death is conjugal—
Lover lying grasses wan
Almost as interjacent bone.

Egregious lust interrogates
The loins' forgotten postulates,
Curious passion scuttles down
The alleys where the eyes are gone.

Beneath the body's lewd embrace
Twists October's present grass;
And at the nostrils of the lover,
Quietly, the wind-seeds hover . . . .

Spain, 1937

Final Spring

OF GRASS, insurgent bud aware,
We in the loop of sudden spring,
Trammelled by tangled green and song
Nostalgic on the ear,
Thrown by the lariat of sun
Are branded with initialled fear.

Between the brazen daffodil
Sprawling headlines through the park,
Between the question on the wind,
On lintels of the hill,
And storage in the hollow tree
Joy adds a hasty codicil.

For we are the muscled living, therefore
Make a hasty signature,
Dispossess the urgent root,
Certify the heir:
Fear, in the framework of the wind,
Fear, and the threat of fear, and fear.

London, 1939

"S.S.R., LOST AT SEA."—*The Times*

WHAT HEAVE of grapnels will resurrect the fabric
Of him, oceans drag, whereof he died,
Drowning sheer fathoms down, liquid to grab on—
Sucked by the liner, violence in her side?
Of no more sorrow than a mottled Grief
In marble. There, fantastic in the murk,
Where saltwhite solitary forests leaf,
He swings: the dark anonymously works.
For who shall count the countless hands and limbs
In ditch and wall and wave, dead, dead
In Europe: touch with anguished name and claim
And actual tear, what must be generally said?
O let the heart's tough riggings salvage him,
Only whose lengths can grapple with these dead.

S.S. *Athenia*
September 3, 1939

On the *Struma* Massacre

Now as these slaughtered seven hundreds hear
The vulgar sennet of thine angel sound,
Grant, in thy love, that they may see that ground
Whose promised acres holy footsteps bear.
For they of only this made credulous prayer—
Even for whom thy Son the tempest bound
And waters walked O not those same where, drowned,
Driven by plausible tongues and mute despair,
These faithful roll! No not as they, with board
And spike, who took Thy sweetness then, do we—
Studied in ignorance, and knowing Thee.
For Thine archaic crown of thorns and cord,
Statistics are become Thine agony,
The ocean designate, Gabbatha, Lord.

February 25, 1942

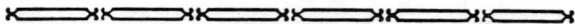

At the *Pinakothek* **Ruins: Munich**

CONSEQUENTLY
Destroyed, all man's good things.
Savonarola yelled
Against creation,
Beauty out of flesh,
Out of dust, perfection.
In the bonfire
Glories curled to ashes
At Firenze.
Eloquent,
The hooked-nose monk,
The thunder,
That set himself alight.
Charred rubies burn brighter.
Think
Who is the better.

So, dumped, the bombs.
Ach, so!
On London,
Munich, down
Where the birds sing
Naming the ruins.
Man bears just so much ecstasy,
And thunders in his cowl.

The Concrete Shall Outlast Us

AND THERE SHALL BE beauty alone in that end
Desolation, the last red rock in the last
Of the sun, the offshore beating on that final
Cliff, a broken spar on the tide. Man
Gone, the earth's grace will be left,
Man and his lash of life gone, elegant
Man, slim limb and eyelash and her
Waiting. A dry weed bends in the wind.
Nothing but the barren.

Against a hinge the door drags. No laughter,
But there has never been laughter. Paper flaps
At the gate. A tooth-broken comb in the dried
Mud. Solitude without use and promulgation,
Only the headland in the reddened light
And going down, the still burning sun.

IV Fire on Stone

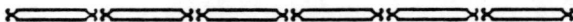

Atlantic Crossing

MUCH have we heard of the false and insecure:
Sunblind blade in the black the grudging fields
At ploughing, zigzag to plummet the hodman builds
His wall, the blackbird on the vulnerable bough.

Unnatural the hands O the touch of lovers downdark,
The fallacy of memorable hills and moon, not fearing—
Galileo at a midnight lens staring
At critical stars: Europe at his back.

On this island-isolation what crag the plunging
Anchor of our fear to drag at? what ambush for the ear,
To intercept the eye what hurdle where, ranging
The whole the windswept glory of the sea? How,
O how this falsehood till final waters the changing
Bone return, gentle denial here?

Flight into Darkness

We have fulfilled our apprehension, hope,
Matched our hands' delay against the sun,
Against a guttering candle written dreams.
Was it today we fumbled spiral of spring,
Clutched at the throat the knot of accurate winds,
Noose and thong by beauty slung?

Yesterday yesterday! the hills were bare of snow,
The hackneyed maple broke with leaf, the bough
Sprang colour along the sweetened air—whose action
Pledged our anger. O we have sworn our lives
Between the hyphened prologue of the crow,
The crimson coming of the rose!

Who now, regretting June with adult smiles,
Set nodding with a finger Buddha's porcelain head:
Hearing of marvels in the township, turned
Expensive keys against the empty street,
From possible cars saw moon eclipse the sun,
Cautious glass before our eyes.

And all that year the tamarack was green
And we who saw the tolerant seed and snow,
By leaning questions ambushed. Grace was then
The grateful turning-out of lamps at night,
Within the book the treacherous flower's clue,
The short escape of perjured love.

For we remembering our defense refused
The mirror's prosecution, praised the speaker
On the chairman's right: within the files,
Found brief anger for the anonymous clock,
Looking up, the calendar on startled walls—
Withdrawing truth from blundering sleep.

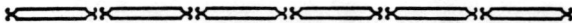

We have waited important letters from the west,
In evening cities heard the newspaper tossed
Against the door, under the prosperous valley
Guessed at oil, proved the legend false.
We dream wisely who once had loved too well.
And yet, coming on sun across

An alien street, stand suddenly surprised—
As Galileo, before his midnight window,
Cloak about his shoulders, coldly chose
A fatal planet—first, listened while
The solitary wagon passed along the road—
Then aimed his contradictory lens.

The Courtyard

THE COURT
Changes light.
Between the backs of buildings
Snow falls swiftly.
The sills of windows
Looking out on winter,
The white pavements,
Are without recall
Or observance
Or terror.
Death
Takes significance:
Edmund the Prince called-to,
Persepolis and all the helpless kings,
Héloise
Taking off her pale blue dress.

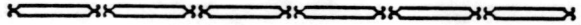

Agamemnon's Mask

FLATTENED, beaten out,
The mask of gold.
But an earlier king, they say,
Miscalled by Schliemann
Digging around, over-anxious,
His mind on windy Troy
And that return to Argos'
Scented bath—
Some Achaean king,
Loved, I suppose,
Who also had children,
Was important,
As the rest of us,
Eating the red bean,
Digesting the day,
Without legend,
Praying the gods,
Without much hope,
Then dying:
The gravesmith,
Out of love,
Beating the fine gold,
The drained face laid away,
Without much trouble,
Without complication,
Without much trouble to anyone.
No matter.
Let it be Agamemnon's.

Agamemnon's Palace

ARGOS, the guide tells us, is famous
For melons. What had he, Agamemnon,
To do with melons! At night, the blood-red
Sun cool in the shadowed porch,
He spit black seeds at table,
Clytemnestra irritated
By his habit? What have we?
Melons are melons. Not significances.
The night of that return, hot
From the shore, the Argive got another
Fame. We're told he held at his lips
An apple: neither feast nor fast,
Dead before he ate it. His fame
Is Clytemnestra's fury.

                    Melons!
Let's hear no more of melons! The kitchen's
Bin is silly with them. There
Are other things than demonstrable pips.

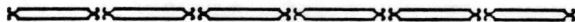

Old Lady Seen Briefly at Patras

THE STICK firm, a short
Crosspiece on top, each side
The hands control the gift of earth
To walk back to her door.
Sixty years back she lay naked
To be loved, thighs the width of him.
But the walk is on cobbles,
Not too good at best, not
With bent spine and incontinence.

Aphrodite's laugh was certain
(*These are reliable reports*),
Not too loud; derisive, but lovely.

Lyric Sarcastic

Star-tons loosed on open eyes,
Forearm up, bruise blind:
Burst midnight thunders down the wind
And wheel of cellared ear. Advise.

What brink and bastion bound can make
Against the common sea delays
Of dart and dazzle, crumple rake
Of sun off ocean's cornice, rays?

Tell what word shall plug the gap
Of wind between the bud's explosion,
The naked petals' proposition
And the breath, collusion stop?

WHEREAS the linkèd verb and brain:
Shall spectacles conches then collect
To glue in numbered cases, maniacs
Acorns pick for pipes to pull on?

Shuffle to mummied pharaohs the pack
Of pips! Yea, we are dupes and dust.
By sun and Sirius double-crossed!
Between our gums Golgotha's crust!

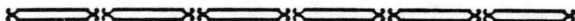

Aspects of Some Forsythia Branches

WAITING for these dry sticks in a vase—
Cut (*with deliberate shears taken*
From the third drawer down on the left) from the bush
In snow—complicated with leaf
And yellow in the earth elaborated, even
In the wintering sun; as the spiral of a protein
Divides and duplicates the thrust
Of love, the hereditary nose of Caesar,
Alexander's brow and Jennie's
Mole; the aggregation of a galaxy!:
So the April science of a bunch
Of sticks cut for an etched glass vase—
Waiting for these to flower in a March
Room—waiting for all this business—
As an act of love, a science of gravel,
A suffering, is this not done
With reliance? One way, dry sticks
Lead to buds, presumably wanted,
To yellow eventually. What trivial aspects
Can be got! We handle love
For small purposes. Yet they serve.
Shrubs are cut for what is believed in.
Somewhere death's in it. Dignity
Is demanded even for the dead.
So we cut branches two
Days ago. Take great precautions.
Go carefully through a door. Stand
Among deathbeds as though among heroes,
Pausing in winter along windy corridors
With the knowledge ahead of us, to wrap our throats.

Black Holes and Beethoven

for Harold Schonberg

BLACK HOLES in heaven and Beethoven
In his room, the broken strings of the piano
Shouting deafness, the meadows somewhere
Out the window, beyond the stair,
Notebook, theme and error, on
His knee, eardrum, hammer silent
Which was no news—he almost,
Tapped, punctured, drained, half
A step from heaven. Meanwhile, Karl,
Juniper tea and the Tenth in his head—
Upstairs black holes turning
Inside out back to eternity
Again. God is His own question.

A canon against mortality:
Das Thor dem Todt: Note hilft.
Note hilft auch aus der Not.

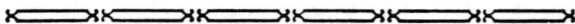

Trio for Harp and Percussion

I   *Argument*

IF GOD is the speed of light,
As well crack walnuts set
At table. If so,
Golgotha is an abstract thought
And Light's speed dug in toes
And shoved a plane at Nazareth.

I'll have the concrete.

From here
To there, quicker than a wink.
There, where's there?
Infinitum. Einstein,
Asked, fiddled. So
Do I. I'll have a measure of music,
A bolt of good concordance,
Heard notes,
Above ground.
Lay me down in time
I'll think of speed.

Light, Erigina's Light
(*Capital L*)'s
An abstract absolute.
I'll have sun
On cranky crystal, corners in
The glass, tablecloths and silver,
Oranges with peels on them,
Crack inconsequential nuts
And talk of music,
Haydn; light my own
Apocalyptic candle.

II *Adagio ma non troppo*

As who shall sit in the sun
Thinking himself immortal,
Rameses in his chair,
His face broken, Tiye
That Nubian queen come
To Egypt done by the sculptor
In jasper hardest after
Diamond, beauty gone,
Only lips left,
The reach of river, dust.
The barge she sat in, like a
Burnish'd throne . . . . Starry
Cassiopeia, lady
With her mirror in
The sky where physics sits
Dispensing laws. I'll
Have earthly music, heard,
Unsphered, no choirs squeaked
In eternal passacaglia
As the planets turn
In need of oil but mortal
Tribulations, that *Festspiel*
Seat hard on the bottom
For sweet acoustics' sake,
Wagner delving his gold
E^b, and sweeter, Schubert
Dying of Eros, handing
The theme that summer in Steyr
To amiable Krump, his bull-fiddle
Less than immortal, Kathi,
Large blue eyes, thick
Gold tresses, upright in
Her chair while papa gives
A dubious *A*, the short-lived
Schubert full of smiles.

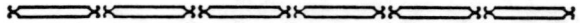

III *Diabelli Variations*

Beethoven's *schusterfleck,* a cobbler's
Patch: magnificence! Sole of a shoe,
Hermes' sandal; skullcap, halo;
Digested mushroom, Helen's shoulder;
Earth a heaven! Well, not quite.
But what the world can do in time!
Transmogrification, mud bedaubed,
Bedizened! Botticelli's girl,
Canvas, paint and camel hair;
James' Bible, glue and ink—
Metamorphosis manipulated
By eardrum, pulse and pate! So,
Diabelli asked Beethoven,
"Ein variation on mein liddle
Theme." Thirty-three! Inanity
Brought sublime, empyrean reached,
Become his last sonata, Beethoven
Deaf!
          Instances, exaltations,
Mortalities—apostrophes at
Their ends! Why not? Any son
Of divinity can rub his nose in dust
If so inclined, a beneficial
Exercise—but not the whole of it,
Fix and finish yet, not
By a longshot, mankind notwithstanding:
Jesus and His lousy deal,
Jonah ducked, Pound pitched
In a loony bin and Liszt betrayed—
The Saturday sundry of this world,
Schumann mad, hearing A,
Schubert turned to the wall to die.

Husks and blossoming, sun and mud.
No help for it.
Ear-trumpets against the stars.

Out of Chaos, His Starry Structures

AND AS GAUDIER saw a cat in uncut
Marble, read a Chinese
Glyph at sight, "It's a horse,"
So that-one and the other-one drew a line
Out of the fine clear air and wrote it down,
The silk and britches of Arden Woods,
The halls of Luxor, in it.

Where did Daphnis cut his tune?
Fuller rest his dome?
And as that firebrand touched the lips of Logos,
Eliot took the word, Yeats his phrase,
Out of all tradition Pound his book.

A star-shell over the Western Front, Gaudier.
Break no ointments,
Out of stone
An "arrangement of surfaces" comes.

The Shuttered Dawn

THE GREAT MAN comes to his finish ninety
Times, capable of nothing more,
Sunset is as the sunset that
First day; tomorrows, accomplished
As much as can be hazarded on one throw,
The farthest possibilities of triumphant
Lens and slide. I think of Gaudier
Killed on the front in '17
The future of sculpture carved in the wood
Of the rifle-butt, all he had
Before the shrapnel closed his throat;
Titian, for ninety years each portrait
His last. Born to greatness is the man
Who sees his skull:

                    Again that pool
Is come to that the torrent splashed to rainbow—
That love is made whose finish was all
That there was though morning was at the shutter
Stars that night would be held by.

Legend

Whoever is washed ashore at that place—
Many come there but thrust by so fierce a sun
The great cliffs cast no shadow, plunge a passage
Inland where foliage and whistling paradise-birds
Offer comfort—whoever has got up,
Standing, certainty under his adjusting heels
And height tugged by the tide, ocean rinsing
From flank and belly, ravelling loins with wet,
Whoever has stayed, solitary in those tropics,
The caverns of his chest asking acres,
                                    he,
Doomed in that landscape but among magnificence,
By shell and seafoam tampered with, his senses
As though by her of Aeaea used, exquisite—
He, that salt upon his time's tongue,
Knows, standing the margin ocean and sand,
Ilium toppled thunder his ears, what's left
Of Helen naked drag between his toes.

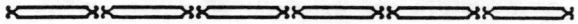

Excelling the Starry Splendour of This Night

EXCELLING the starry splendour of this night,
What link and lash that bind my bones
I think of now amazed whose hinge
Was even in seed articulate.

Or even on this sharp and dreadful edge
Of death my eyes lift up and see
Against the tug and tangent of
Our going, the centred stars.

Slow wheel the crackling heavens hung within
The pinpoint of an eye, my ear
Is sensible and whorls archaic
Music in its round.

Look how the architecture of this night
Is scarp and scaffold for an inch
Of breath and all its glory margined
By a breadth of palm!

Whereby what mortal crevice, coign of skull
Shall man be less, than all, this whole
And aggregate of god; snuff
With a pinch of logic, proof?

And he was fashioned in the sight of god,
That sits in conclave with his clock
Denial in his loins. He shall
This day surely plant turnips,

Fiddle with a shoestring: tomorrow serve
A grasp of gravel with his deeds.
O death, denied by every shoveller
Of dirt whose wage is love,

Come cranking, then, to him, test-tube, text,
Within thy claw. No man that's sneezed
But will from all thy groans and gravings
Pluck the paradox!

Go tell the lips of lovers kiss a skull;
The loin athletic, fathers dust!
The great earth turns. The heavens move.
Orion bends his bow.

Mighty night and firmament of glory
Here, on the *yes* of an eyelid hung!
The broad hills break whereon you stand,
Man of god who gave.

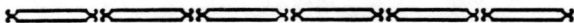

Among the Wheatfields

THE SKY had amplitude, so had the great fields.
I had difficulty in claiming the sky so wide was
The horizon. So windswept was the grass
I stood there, a probable of contemplation
In the wideness of eternity. My heart was small, it is four
Inches across, but I knew the directions found there,
I knew in its compass was all I needed to know
Of width, of limits farthest from supposition:
The progress of wind in the stalks, the wheatspears
Rust-colour, the rasp of a particular love.
I awaited the final knowledge of knowing,
The consolidation of eternity, yet what I knew,
The place where I was wholly, was already what
Those absolutes are. The trouble of final
Exaltation, this fieldwork finished with,
The going, was still given over to that which I would
Not have: completion, joy without desire,
The whole field done with that is joyful death.

Green Disposition

THE WORLD'S a green world. The phlox is red:
Against the stone wall brilliant the clusters
Stand out appointing the grey and green of
Cedar hedge and wall—counterpoint
Of His brilliance, the garden in His mind
When thrown were primal suns, green
Assertions. Looked up from this vantage, the hill
And trees and hedge and lawn are green, only
Birch tree, bark white, is against
This ordering, this green world, enclosing round
Red rose and saffron marigold
And yellow rose arranged not by God
This time but proof of how this shambles
Of magnificence when brought to arbitration
By our love is provident enough
Of joy. In this garden-world of scraps
Of God, the world is green. The claim of snow
Is only time's matter, no dominion.
Scarlet phlox and stone affirm green.

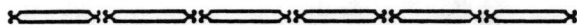

Anniversary

AND AT ten minutes to four
The sun broke through—only
For about a moment but long enough
To set once more aflame the maple.
Gold struck crimson and I knew
Life shaped and shaken; the sun,
Leaves falling (*a chill wind*
With rain all day), across the land
And lake and uncertain hedge,
Gold struck and I thought: So,
Eternity tumbles, oak, maple,
Once valid counter since spring
Was pledged—yet, burned through the mist,
There is the sun, there is the sun!
Affirmation for the moment
Was a falling leaf (*Akhenaten banished*
Gods until there was only worshipped
Sun; let sun burst and
We too worship). Only a moment—
But our attachment made, leaves
Fell without their season, gold
Struck angles of the cornice,
Marvel was as it was.

Where Leaves Have Fallen

HILLS ENCLOSE the lake;
the hour of sun, a silver
over hills,
is acclamation,
trees down to the water are bare,
winter
its own acceptance,

the hour enters the last of this landscape.

Not the years that are come,
not the seasons brought to conclusions,
harm the hour.

Stone steps where leaves have blown
are small barriers.
The brown apples have fallen.

Leaves, brown apples,
brought down,

these,
these perceived,
are all that is needed:
brown is fallen across silver,
accumulations of ripeness
happen.

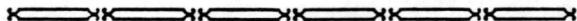

Spring Night

ALL is one
Out of this sensuous news!
A million stars, the skies
Spill silver metaphysics,
The moon
Golden logic throws.
Massawippi's silver!
Atum, I call!
First Flamboyance,
Immensity,
Self-loved,
Owing nothing,
He
Whose throw of glory
Drenched the elemental seed.

V In Dispraise of Great Happenings

Carta Canadensis

THE LAND starts *dentelle*, indented,
With tidemark of hills, broadens
Into dark green canting
Over rock eternal with loneliness,
Northwestward tilting from granite
The ochre lakes. This
Is the great Shield clamped
On the place of love. Only
At the tide and inland littoral
Is there literal love. Wharves
Wash on the waves of wheat
Husky with summer luck,
In autumn harvested on the plains.
Fish and wheat, the promise,
Christ and bread,
Brought to the tables of
An iron land.
           Backward
Up against the possible
East, the broken mountains
Of magnificence
Sheering the plainsoil northward
Out of sight, roses
Lean, provincial, burning
In their plot.

Wednesday at North Hatley

IT SNOWS on this place
And a gentleness obtains.
The garden fills with white,
Last summer's hedgerow
Bears a burden and birds
Are scarce. The grosbeak
Fights for seeds, the squirrel
Walks his slender wire.
There is a victory;
The heart endures, the house
Achieves its warmth and where
He needs to, man in woollen
Mitts, in muffler, without
A deathwish, northern, walks.
Except he stop at drifts
He cannot hear this snow,
The wind has fallen, and where
The lake awaits, the road
Is his. Softly the snow
Falls. Chance is against him.
But softly the snow falls.

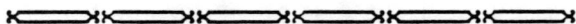

Quebec Night

THE RED LOGS
crisp on the outside,
the wood solid, being new,
are chained to the sleigh.
The runner drags a cleat for the hill up,
and the snow is pleated in the logs,
the snow in the far woods
falling

Quebec Sugarbush

SO IMMINENT the earth's returning
No critical snow of winter now
But islands snag of soil.

The iron forest's fearful peace
Numbers the armament of summer,
Mutiny of sun.

Something more than signature
(*The huge sedition of the hills*)
To sterile peace:

The close conspiracy of hollows
At the brittle ribs of snow,
The broken pool

And talk of men in iron woods
Native to the inviolate blood.
At strangled maples

Where buckets are sweet with sap drives
Telesphore of the crimson tuque
His barrel from pail to tree.

Quebec Winterscene

AND THE SNOW trodden round the yard,
Soiled with boots and fetched cordwood,
Straw ravelled near the barn—
The long snow of the fourfold land.
At dusk, acres clamped cold,
Threshold and clearing everywhere white
To the distant scribble of alders, across
The frozen field snakefence
Like charred music; sky only harvest
Helps over, buckled, with taste of tin
Dipper icy a man drinks gasping,
Sweat of warm barn-work a hazard
Once out, door-to, headed for house.

At eight, night now pitch, the train,
Halted for mailsacks at the swung
Lantern—the far horizontals
A moment, a history happening
The hills—alongside, pants, monstrous,
Pistons poised.   Then pulls past.

At the cutting, heard warning

                    whose only
Answer is the local heart.

Country Walking

I

Two humps of snow stood on two fir trees,
The place looked like an entrance to importance,
To a field of white snow, field
As in heraldry, leading nowhere of much
Consequence, a slope with a cottage on it
Shut up for the winter, the roof without icicles,
No one there for a fire. I went between the gates
Of the trees to anywhere. Shadows on the slant
Were purple, prints were in the snow
For no purpose, the denizen apparently
Not caring, going on instinct.
I thought of sophistications, music and poems:
How Liszt solved his fugue
Back into romantic grandeur,
How Yeats shook the desert birds
With emerging beasts of Bethlehem.
The snow was darkening white,
Runnels of shadow unravelling.
It seemed consequence was forgotten.
I looked back then upward, to ominous clouds.
I went on across the hastening light,
My weight pressing in, leaving
Footprints, a complication into.
Suddenly
Sun slammed through going.

II

As you go up the road you will notice
That not all the trees are slapped
With snow on the north bark-side,
The south wind up the lake
Is also bitter on days that are not
Still, redpolls feed on the road
Only with ruffled comfort. Farther
Up the hill you will look at
Caps of snow undisturbed
On the upright posts of the snakefence
Slants. The hill here is protected
By a higher rise of fir and bare
Aspen. As you go down, slowly
Black Point swings by and the lake
Appears. The spread snow on the ice
Is formally patterned by the wind in strokes
Of parallel shade as if some purpose
Was meant. Farther on, just
To the side of you on the white snow open
To sudden sun, green and crimson
Crystals flash, too trivial
To matter, blue also and where red
Impinges, a purple not having
Any regal purpose evident
But the whole refraction so dazzling,
The white and jewelled field,
You raise your eyes. You can always look
Away. The wind here slaps
The cheek and forehead with cold again.
Farther on there is a red barn.
An outdoor double wooden swing
Belongs to the landscape, the apple-barrel
Is tipped over beside the tree,

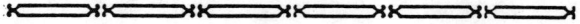

An abandonment of no use. Beyond,
The place you had headed for proves
Upland too exposed to go to.
You will turn home but notice how
The shadows now hard on the crust
Are broken crossing the ploughed road.
The wind at your back seems to have dropped.
The way home, familiar, always
Seems shorter. The snow creaks.

III

The moon is up there with a cart on it
White-golden. Down here,
Calmly ice on the lake freezes;
The movement of air brushes the cheek
With cold; old Mr. Hall is dying.
There is no concern. Christmastree lights
In places blink green and red
For whatever purposes Eaton's makes of it.
My nose wants to run. Gloves on,
I wait to get home. I want to get home
To my own true love. It is glorious.

Prologue to Summer

QUICK at the maple's root
The woodchuck garbles leaves,
Flung from its tooth
Flake of sun.

Under the gangrened stump
Slugs drag slime,
The fieldmouse gnaws
The crust of air.

Smell!—the leaf-mould smokes,
At the water-edge flapped
By the waves a fish
Belly-up stinking.

Soil thaws. The ice
Rotted from broken wharf
Where last-year's coin
Is silver gotten.

Male-naked the air. Compel!
Urgent the deed, urgent
And muscular the dream
Invaginate!

The Moment Is Not Only Itself

RAKING LEAVES, putting them in bags,
Stooped over, green gloves on—
The whole of it suddenly Chopin's Prelude
In E♭ major. You know it? *Vivace.*
Legato e sempre leggiero?
Difficult, intricate, melody
As outside the possibility of this world
Of heaviness as want of it. Not
Ache of muscles of the wrists unused to the
Stretches put me in mind of it.
Shoving leaves into tilted bags
Is easy enough, no strain on what
Fingers can do though not brought
To sensitive answer by a lifetime's agony—
That is, joy—the same thing,
The music gained thought worth it; or
Those hands, width, stretch, joint,
Apart from what sheer will can bring them
To, actually physiologically
Born to eighty-eight keys of such
And such a width and space, astoundingly
Matched to the world's manufactury.
Not to be accounted for, miracles. I
Leaned over to get autumn in bags
And suddenly it was April. It
Was October, almost the end of it.
Air was gentle up from the lake,
It smelled of branches, there was a crow's caw,
The sun was hot. It was spring; so.
Perhaps that was the craziness brought Chopin
In my head, that Prelude when
The year was finished. Affiance fools
The brain. As in love often.
What is real is what the heart
Has. Old leaves in green

Bags are beginnings with the wind right,
Chopin in your head. What chose
To have it there is your own doing.
My guess is the way senses
Are lived. Not to deny autumn
Its own glory, dead leaves
Affirming April are what you've loved
Brought to bear: high mindings,
Signals of thought, code of body
Made exquisite and tall doings,
Structures of beauty that make end
Of foliage, of summer, descendings, however
You finish it, not matter.

In Dispraise of Great Happenings

Birdsong and the midge drinking needfully:
Otherwise happenings of summer afternoons.
Such great fountains tumble water
At d'Este. I at the spring unwanted
At the corner of the patio, my foot in it
Unobserved, pull weeds. The choice
Between weedy violet and potential
Ground-phlox massed in May and red
And white and to be propagated, is Troy
Fallen or not, a thing of moment
And momentous choice whether the midge succeed
In swallowing smaller than itself, or
Should birdsong cease? Let Helen
Waddle down the street and be beautiful.
I shall go to bed far later on
And pull the sheet up over time.
Now I watch the cataclysmic gulp
By midges made and conjugate
What question lies in oriole song
Oblivious of Agamemnon and a thousand ships.

Garden Information on Behalf
of Hummingbirds

Red trumpet-shaped flowers,
Not only to match the long tongues
But to lessen competition of bees,
And red since hummingbirds
See blue less well. Energy
Burnt at such a rate, ruby
Throats must hibernate at night.

This for those who love them. More:
They hover, therefore plant blossoms
Accordingly, pendulous fuchsias
For instance, rich in nectar, without
The landing platforms bee-flowers
Have, winter mint is good,
Jewelweed and spiderflower.

They love to sip in sunshine beebalm
And columbine, coralbells
And *phlox divaricata* for those
With latin. Fragrance or lack of it
Is of no consequence. Among the vines
And shrubs, the scarlet runner bean
Is fine, beautybush and lilacs.

All this for a flash of colour hardly.
Preferably include a wall which
In itself can be attractive and occupies
Little space while holding up flowers.
A succession of blossoms up to the last
Of August is to be thought of, then
The birds head south. Frost threatens.

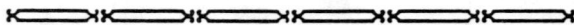

Allhallows Eve

UNTIL THE DUST from the broom came
In the beam from the basement window
The suncast was invisible. It squared
Tangled. The smash on the far wall
Hit cement low down since the sun
Stood high over the next house
And the elm at the roadway. Crammed
With dancing dust, anywhere near it
Man sneezed.

        The ladder was put
Away, halloween was on
The doorstep, the second day All Souls.
Lucifer! he shouldn't have fallen to Satan.
The beam was glorious, dust in it,
Autumn leaves were raked and the bulbs
In, the gates to Eden open,
No one needed to climb walls.

At Moraine Lake

CANADA, a country without myths.
We need none. I sit by the fire
And let my native wit buzz,
Here in the cabin by the lake,
The whole of Hybla's in this hive—
The walk round Babel to Consolation
Lake, our boots set out to dry,
Wet from trying to get to Quadra—
Circe's weed and bedstraw,
Flowers which grew on a bank that stand
Now in a milkjug above on the mantel
The fire beneath, that wouldn't let
The morning off—dry feet
And love sum it up—I meant
The boots as narrative, not Odysseus
Smelling somewhat of the heat—
But let them stand, I can think
Of comprehension such that jug
And square-nailed boots are Philomela
Snowbound. The plumbing in the kitchen
Shakes the roof, my love cooks beans—
Almost I could get what I drive at down
To beans but stick at hoodwink, ketchup
Being bloody Oedipus. We'll go
To bed later and be our ghosts
And pull the gravel over. Being's
More instructive. I make coffins
For alarm clocks with it and think
Of history: Plantagenet, a piece
Of broom to sweep the kindling out
(*Caesar calked to keep the winds
Away*). My mind gets smart on brambles—
Plantagenet's a plant. Passion
Is instructed from itself.
I bend here in the dark and get

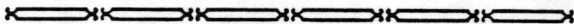

More fire up, as I shift the birch
The flames break out. Myths lie
About us in our infancy.
Take her of the foam somewhere where
It's warmer. Look, I am occupied with
The irrevocable decisions of the ants.

The Walk in Yoho Valley

WE SET IN for the Twin Falls.
This is in the Yoho Valley,
Yoho, meaning wonderful.
Up the lanky delta, the first
Hitch dumped us sunward onto
Forest level. The state of the world
At this time was not good:
All men were dying. We had come up
The surest way, each foot
Alternately ahead. Mountains
Tipped over morning, treetrunks
Trimmed the sun to dazzle, we tripped
On ragged dapple, stopped to sort
The propaganda. Bett saw three
Scotomas go up Whaleback Mountain,
They looked like Klee (*Canadians
Are pedestrian in shape,
Not likely to be on whaleback that
Far inland*). What I saw was Miro.
She said she heard them yodel. Miro's
Spanish. I took her by the hand,
Away from dazzle. We went into
The forest. Everywhere was green,
Green and silence, on each hand;
Under cool cliff, corridor.
I dallied in God—inexplicably,
Since I was happy. Deer drank dappled.
More miles we went there
In trees, and there was Laughter Falls
Cold as all get-out among green,
Pounding down paeans from high up,
Hurl held, then down lashed
Hitting the boulders with good wash.
But this was big. There were immeasurables:
Lousewort and pinchmoss

Detaining stars, stipples of sticks,
Bark wrinkles and root loops
And other things thrown around,
As birds' wings, beetles' backs,
And snails' glens; flies in fine
Fettle, butter- and dragon-, wobbled
And stood over streams and blossom.
Gravely elk grazed, antlered.
Gorgeous glades ranked river.
We had dark chocolate under glaciers,
Squares of it, eating for energy.
Everything was up now, high
Hauls and switchbacks, rivers
Canyoned. Trail-marks were good,
This being complex country.
Forests filled in. Trolltinder
Was gone, a whole glacier, though cold
Came. Pines groped greatly
For airspace. We clung on cliff-
path, down there Yoho
Marbled and moulded between banks.
Nothing was dawdle. This was a curt
Climb, no breath was sloven
And there was no talk, nothing small.
Stones, round stones were what
We watched; scenery was footpath.
One judged. And there was Twin
Falls! Two miles and roaring.
In between trees. Half
A hundred feet falling, great water,
White! Two miles we tugged,
Up, taking breath, beholding—
Till we came on clearing. It
Was fine faring, finally, under
Ice, and green granting, the log
Latch giving, and fresh tea.

In the Coast Range

SNOWCRESTS were flung around us,
Fresh snow since last night,
Mountains dazzling in the sun,
The Skeena, wide here, below the dazzle,
Catching the shapes, the snow twice;
The railway along the edge, the road
To the ocean, the coast of timber and salmon
And wheat for Asia; the window of the coach,
The car corridor toward the south,
Toward the crests of snow, too low
If you were to stand, for them to be seen;
You knelt, you had to kneel if you were to have
The peaks, the actual grandeur
Above the reflection in the still water,
The river from the glaciers above.
You had to get down for that, kneel.
But that was the thing to do.

In the Yukon

IN EUROPE, you can't move without going down into
    history.
Here, all is a beginning. I saw a salmon jump,
Again and again, against the current,
The timbered hills a background, wooded green
Unpushed through; the salmon jumped, silver.
This was news, was commerce, at the end of the summer
The leap for dying. Moose came down to the water edge
To drink and the salmon turned silver arcs.
At night, the northern lights played, great over country
Without tapestry and coronations, kings crowned
With weights of gold. They were green,
Green hangings and great grandeur, over the north
Going to what no man can hold hard in mind,
The dredge of that gravity, being without experience.

VI Aesthetics at Delphi

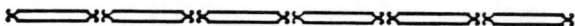

The Bronze Doors at Pisa

TALLER than two monks, the bronze doors at Pisa,
In one oblong the angel of the Lord on Jesus' sepulchre
Swinging his feet. Hammerwork
Sophisticated with innocence
More in love with heaven than chapels of rococo
Florid with space.
Lord, deliver us!
Anonymity, simpleness and faith.

The Mori: Venezia

THE UNADVISED would think these four sculptured brothers
Attached to St. Mark's
Were the Babes in the Wood. They clutch each other
As though leaves were falling
And in their cloaks they would lay them down
Amid the cathedral of trees
The sun shining through
In one spot like the great burnished blade
Of Michael
Golden and glorious, the glance of God,
While the birds cover them forlorn
From the thin hot
Scimitars of Saladin flashing around
Jesus' tomb.
But they're not:
They're gazing dismayed
At Othello's snotrag dropped
On the *piazzetta* as
He sweeps mad
Up the stairs.
They're out of tune,
Being born in the 4th century.
They sing "*Willow*" for comfort.
One has lost a porphyry foot.
They guard the cathedral
But they are cornered:
Christians embrace one another:
The Sunday afternoon with the doves
Goes up in a madness of colours.
Their four swords seem extra.
The Wicked Uncle in the dark woods, poking the leaves,
Picks final mushrooms.

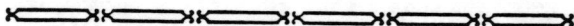

The Horses of Saint Mark's

Had virgin
Such beautiful feet?
Ha! hoofs!
Placed on their pedestals,
One forefoot up,
Nostrils snared in the Venetian wind.
Had ever such flanks mistresses
Certain enough?
Stabled, these four,
Collared and clipped,
Though who
Had them?
What groom
For the rippled strength?
One hoof
(*Should he turn*)
Through the shattered mosaics,
Gadded by the thought
Of foam
On Poseidon's thundered sands.

Mausoleum Hunting: Ravenna

THEODORIC the Emperor,
One night, the lid off,
Was dispersed by
A little wind.

The Philosophy of the Parthenon

PROPORTION is all things of beauty.
Dimension, go beyond dimension,
Calculation, measure nothing,
Only in relation, the cornice balanced
Against the line, the line against
The truth, not as an existence
But as a meaning, the marble line
The respect to itself, the incumbent gods.

Aesthetics at Delphi

HER STRAY DRESS
    and sea-blue eyes
askance
    (*O Corinth-blue waters*)
her legs bare
    crotch for a fish-smelling youth

    Pythia, chewer of bay-leaves!
    a propoundment for you here

a disturber from nearby Krissos

This at the meeting-place of eagles

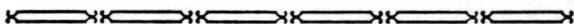

At the Odeum of Herodes Atticus: Athens

So Agamemnon barefoot
On the scarlet rug,
Ten years, from Troy,
Cassandra in his chariot,
Entered Mykenai.

Silence, silence,
Beyond that door.

What ablutions
Bring on the times?
What times shall end
With that red bath?

A wail as of winds
In the towers . . . .

Barefoot, red-cloaked,
Agamemnon, royal,
The royal Agamemnon,
Barefoot against his nature,
Enters Mykenai.

On the Bull-Leapers' Fresco: Knossos

TOSSED by the swart bull
these Minoans play.
Death, the sleek coat
twitched and teased, groomed
for his own purpose, hoofs
pared, horns gilt,
is, lust for the belly, the silver
gut, jumped over.
The point is to change
that two ton lift
into parabolas of air.
The fifth time, the perfect
touch, turned-over, hands
to the coarse hair, heels
to sand—you are master of.
Sweat and the sweat of bull,
you love. Defecation
compels and death
is useful.
Than the assault, the danger is
to love the last time.

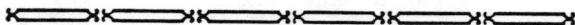

Four Exaltations for Sea-Shell,
Pulley, Pan Pipes and Golden Clarion

1

Poseidon, seagod of the white-foam horses—
And all the gods believed-in!
Sounion, there lies Sounion!
White marble above the drenched blue sea.
High, the marble cliff-hung—
(*Not blooded crossed limbs*
Hung lugubrious, sackcloth around His
Swag)—hauled marble from
Pentelikon, set in order, column
Dedicated, the god revered,
Above the turbulent sea!

2

Poseidon! Poseidon! What if he
Should? walk down this theatre
Dripping seaweed, trident
Propped on shoulder, a coddy smell,
Nothing on, shocking the ladies
Of the Eastern Townships. Ah, a mighty
Choice. On the one hand,
At any time, snuffled salt
And earthquakes, the seagod,
His pillars wind-slapped white;
On the other, Friday: indoor
Crepe and paraphernalia;
Come Monday: pious washing
Hung along fleecy gullible lines.

3

The myrrh tree burst asunder,
Came forth Adonis,
Adonis, his breath as spring,
His youth as peeled hickory.
To Aphrodite, half,
And sweet Persephone, her season,
Zeus apportioned him,
As though the earth
For honey hives and all its fruits
Must wait the snowy sheets
Of dark Persephone and she
The snowy foam
Of lovely Cythera.
Believe no choice between these snows!
Adonis each his province gives
Though winter has no rose
And summer to its answers come.

4

Radiant intelligence, said Kung
(*Old Confucius, still descendent*
In Shantung. But where the silks?
The judge who sits in order?
Only the glint of silk, the sheen,
Sunshaft molten on sleeve,
Shimmer on water).
OMNIA QUAE SUNT
LUMINA SUNT!: Plotinus' plot
To turn the world on: Light!
Bright effluence of

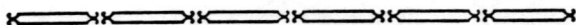

Bright essence increate, acclaimed
Blind Milton with his drop serene.

Light tensile!
With Zagreus, Dionysus
With his lynx smell, old Kung's order,
Turn the world!

Words for a Resurrection

AND UNICORNS broke cover
and all the copse was covered with crocus.
This was in autumn when finches munch gravel
and satyrs acorns
which make them mad.

A queer time, an odd *pendule*
and waggle of pendulum.

But I thought of the crisis of Pan
and the tone of *F* minor when
someone yelled: *Great Pan is dead!*

. . . moss stuffed his ears as he rolled
as he came and he didn't hear.
Sex was more.

Unicorns grazed unafraid of the coming

and all the sunsets blazed in an uprising.

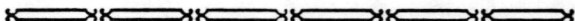

Canto for Pan

Out of his coming paeans ring.
In a circle the snowdrops, already
Under the snow a wheeling of witness
Working for sun. Sun! Buds stiffen
And branches are sticky with sheathing
On petals that thrust and will colour spring!
Still muddy the soil, but crimson
Tipping the shove of peony at top of
The garden steps. Bells hang round
And pendulums wring down scales off the
Male-hung fir. Wind senses
Lapsing of snow-smell now unravelled
As time unravels all things borne.

Nightpiece in Asia Minor

GONE the Aegean sun in orange
Fire. Beyond the bay of Izmir
The gods are fled, all inconvenient
Beauty. The sceptre moon is silver—
Still pursued by its silver star.
Now in the grove at Didyma the broken
Columns cast their length; shadows
At Miletus scatter where once the sea
Came smooth to marble portals, washing
A little, disturbed by Helios' stallions'
Elsewhere splashed halt. Near
The portal's edge, you remember?
Tin glinted, time turned
A spiral spring to rust. And now,
The acropolis of Pergamum; under the moon
Two sacred pine-trees, the hall of Zeus . . .
Take my hand quietly here.
Dripping Poseidon once laughed and passed
Us knowing by, now Zeus his knowledge,
His ravelled moonlight throws. Out
Of ravaged hearing in goat-flocked Pergamum
Far below, the muezzin calls
By microphone Islam to prayer.

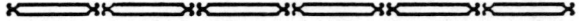

Paestum, That Place of Lovely Temples

THE GREEN-EYED goddess nimble and passionate
Invests this place, Athena in Campania;
Vines and olives her sister Ceres
Looks after. Far cry,
Rome and Saint Peter's worn-down toe!
Here thirty columns drenched two thousand
Years in setting suns support
Nothing. On the *Via de' Fiori* the cripple
Syncopates a cockcrow church;
Down the aisle before a bleeding
Christ mixed up with tourists, suppliance
Raises prayers.

              Contrasts! This
With that. The seasoned heart so
Accepts didactics, sun on marble
Is detraction, opposition
To a penance, the nimble goddess
Soggy substance in the brain.

Atlantis

THE SIMPLE construction, harmony!
Here it was. Plato is witness.
In this wine-red sea,
Atlantis, Santorin to Crete,
The kingdom of all men's better
Minds, justice for innocence,
Joy for children: all negatives,
Marsyas skinned, Christ hung,
Opposing, the flesh-stained wall,
The child struck, surprised: all
Heart-saddening things resolved,
Those known and not known
Among people beautiful to look at,
Gentle, with grace thought well of and rites
Of courtesy, Atlantis, from far Knossos
To Thera—here where the broken cliffs
And fields parched stand above
The widened sea, Akrotiri
Gone. Geology, the crater,
Gone crazy—goodbye to the curls of the ladies,
The gilded bulls. Pumice is
To be picked up at the roadside.
The crust of the globe, plugged, twisted
Until mountains gave and earth trembled
(*Poseidon!*), Knossos gone, Thera—
A thousand walls gone under
The wine-red sea. The drowned
Pillar translucent where the sea
Is still. *Xairete!* The goatherd walks
With his crook the sun and silly melons
Sprawl the desolate field.
                                        Here,
On Santorin, the sun burns,
The stone of cities topples the slope.
Under the shed on the peninsula,

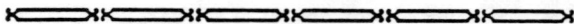

Out of the ash, excavated,
A pot.

In Sight of Etna

Etna, cone of snow. And oleander,
Paths of oleander, pink and sweet-smelling,
Fields of wheat, copper-gold and windblown
Bronze, bronze against green, the green of olive,
Silver-green the Mediterranean; over the island,
Cone of snow. We stand on ashy
Desolation, crust beneath our feet.
Harsh contrast! gods demolished, great Zeus
His temple down that Agrigento built,
The green valley shaken. Empedocles
Leaps in, incinerates himself to show
Himself a god. Lava in Etna winked.
This is greatness. Taormina the pretty,
The unfinished earth molten where Etna shrugs.

The Mosaics, Kariye Djami: Istanbul

THAT PEACOCK crushed in the corner,
Again in blue and deep blue and blue
The folded tail
In swept-up medallion
Studded dusted stars,
Is hoofwork doing:
The Virgin there
Demure
In the vault,
And Joseph's doubt
In the ribs that come together,
Joiner's glue—
But who? who
Had Mary?
Ah, that is
Peacock program,
Asking who.
Faith does it.
Poor old Joseph
In mosaics like his April darling,
Peacock hidden in the groin.
Out with pragmatics!
Uncouple.
Then you have it:
Christ tacked up
And humble Mary
Brought with child.
What! shall peacocks preen
And have their cobs?

Galla Placidia, Empress of the West, Builds Her Tomb: Ravenna

HER HAND touched the wiry hair
   of lovers,
and she passed through the cool rooms
   lovely, they say,
but indifferent to the barbarity;
   night-blue stags
drinking, arcs, stars, vegetables,
   encrusted
in mosaics blue and dark blue
   bent around her tomb
lighted by the vaulted windows closed
   by shaven amber,
these, she passed along painted wood
   corridors to,
come from the white sides of chariot
   drivers, boys,
the roughened beds her expiation for Him
   nailed on heaven,
wearing her hair soft as the air
   doves and peacocks
step through dipping on the path
   red rind of plums;
paled by the honeyed passage of the lovers,
   she came, unsettling
the hand of the artists of Syria on ladders
   beside the snow-cold tomb.

The Resurrection of the Body:
Morning Prayer, Westminster Abbey

SHE HAS GROWN
used to it, that lady.
Preposterous.
Nothing outlandish,
out of line,
the body—only
a spite of the eye,
a rise in the shoulder
hardly noticeable—
not after twenty
years: a slight
limp in the human
kindness lived with
so long
the crash of hurt
is pure silence;
the immaculacy
got used to—
no longer mirrors
are an agony,
the hidden nerve
alive to comment.
All, all
is tranquil, nothing
can be seen
under the voracious pool of the eye,
no lust, no deceit,
either in brain or cell,
no denial and
lubricity,
nothing but a wish
for suppletory
matters, an inch

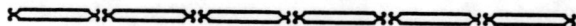

of height, a curly
capillarity,
what is neither
here nor there
really, not
the thin lip,
the pursed mouth,
the grant of
the brow, only
the dearest body
back; the same
returned; her love.
Preposterous, preposterous.

Letter to Akhenaten

You put by the loveliest woman in Egypt
To take up with your brother. You thought
Love was all one and truth so potent
You could make it public. Nefertiti
Went to the North Palace and Smenkhara
The golden boy was surrogate for your own
Ugliness. Misfortune all round. The Window
Of Appearances at which you made everyone
Stand naked in truth before the populace,
Didn't work. The viewers were curious or shocked,
The truth wasn't what should be achieved.
Illusion was, the pun on habit clothed.
Not pot-bellies but rainbows and panoply.
You tried it with God, making Him one,
The one Aten, not cow-eared Hathor,
Horus the night-hawk and Khons with a boat
And moonshine. It was no good, monotheism.
The temple wants diversity, more money in it,
Your sundisk with its rays of little hands
Giving breath to the nostrils, your shining Light,
Wasn't enough though you move a city
Down the Nile. The old alleys are what
Men want, familiar establishments. You know
Where you stand then, not some
Abstract Benevolence up over the horizon
Somewhere. Cover your belly, go back to Thebes,
Give up believing your truth is my truth.
Truth is what is convenient and comfortable.
You can't win the world over with poetry.

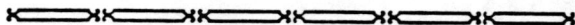

Assisi

THE CORPSE of Santa Chiara
Is black in the face.
A true miracle
Therefore?
Nevertheless they show her.
She saved the city
And was good.

Listen to those birds.
The bushes are liquid with song.
Saint Francis walks truly!
The caged doves skyscape jailbreak making,
The doe adoring,
His hole-hurt breadcrumbed hand
The small birds
A Calvary
Wingthrashing!

VII Armorial

Armorial

I LAY DOWN with my love and there was song
Breaking, like the lilies I once saw
Lovely around King Richard, murdered
Most foully and all his grace at Pomfret,
The roses of England stolen; our love
Was like gules emblazoned at Canterbury
Most kingly in windows and leópards
Passant on bars of gold. This
Was our heraldry.

Our love was larks and sprang from meadows
Far from kingdoms, which regal grew
With rod and bloodred weed and rush
Where water ran; this was our love,
The place where she chose, I could not but come,
A field without myth or rhetoric.
She lay down with love and my hand
Was gold with dust of lily. This
Was our province.

There was song in that kingly country
But I saw there, stuck like a porcupine
On Bosworth Field the arrows through him,
That regal and most royal other
Richard, runt and twitch in a ditch,
His hand wristdeep in lily where
Henry Tudor rolled him, the gules
Of England draining on his shirt.
My love wept.

The Meaning

So I, who love, with all this outward
Now have done, upon each sense
Has purpose inned, the five are sermoned,
Meaning is a prevalence

Not in churches only. There was
A time the world was otherwise,
Sensation had and finished with
And got again nor flesh a guise

That Plato wore. Against the tongue
The tastes of wheat and words were never
Then a scripture; ice was zero;
I did not tremble loving her

Who now, the fool of intellect,
Am hoist with wisdom. Tutelar,
I contemplate a doorknob, prove,
Proclaim like any thunderer.

No sooner love than hell and heaven
Batter at the pagan sense:
My coatsleeve grazes fire; snow,
My elbow jostles permanence;

Within my waiting skull terror
Hunches in a wainscot's mouse;
Where the oak is, the woodbird heedless
Hammers at my final house.

Her Love as a North

THERE IS NOTHING no nothing like it
The pomegranate not set
With the sweet pod split
Nor the carapace of vines,
Full and over,
On the convent wall.
Everything here is sharp
Hard come-by
But deliberate
Like fieldrock brown
Against the turning blade.
Within the deliberation of her love
Her hair is butternut
She has the winter of content,
The need against
The locked white taken.

A Window, a Table, on the North

FROM BLUE to dusk and the lights came.
It was as simple as that
High over the city.
Not as a cry of birds, on wings,
The summer swift green below,
The situation was stone sober.
We were philosophers,
Saw over,
The world wide,
The avenues a distance of arcs
That enclosed like longitudes,
The single point of crossings
The polar night.
Ice came on in the park
A pink rink
And the band blew
Happily
The streets running forever
North and birds flew high
Companions to our honour
And all over dominion
Lights came out.

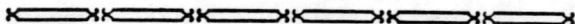

Beach with White Cloud

WE HAVE LAIN by the sea
On the white sand,
And I have spoken
And touched your hand.

You were aware of the seagull
And the wide sky
Shattered by the blue
And the guard and the cry

Of the urchin tugging
Sea-kelp. Your hair
Was darkened and the sun
Seadark there.

The rage touched
Your knees, thighs.
Blood broke, bread,
Stone, skies.

Rustico Beach

THE HUSHING slow break and then
The draw under, again, the hush
Of tide. How quiet the ocean!
Not a footstep, the sand miles,
Only the mark, her walking beside me.
Low on the horizon, the ship
Without commerce with this beach.
The smell of kelp washed by the tide.
Not yet sand, the rocks small
Underfoot at the edge, their meaning
The briefness—of no return ever—
Unheeded, the truth the sound
Of the slow sea and her hand.

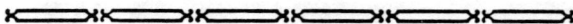

At Mykenai

I pray the gods a respite from these toils
—The Guard, *Agamemnon*

SHE LEANED forward
And smelled the purple flower.
Cyclamen and olive, the dusty olive,
Oleander, the crimson blossom,
Edged the Argive plain;
Up from the broad and rising valley
The Cyclops' walls,
Each stone
Its tons
By those who built at Tiryns
Ramparts for the sea-drenched god,
Impregnable lifted into place.
Mute three thousand years
The chariot rims
That cut the yard;
Nine years since that Atridian pair
Sceptred by shifty Zeus
Sought the windy ramparts
Of lascivious Troy.
Eager hibiscus
Also there was she walked by,
Flower of blood
And hot sex.
The wind blew lightly
And a dust settled against the step.
She turned. The wind touched her hair.
This was where she leaned forward
And smelled the flower,
The Cyclops' wall was,
Hector dead,
And at the Lions Gate,
Agamemnon in his bloody sheet.

The Sun on the Temple Was Gold

NINE YEARS, nine, since we
rode donkeys up to Lindos first.
Light bathes the broken columns,
blue the Aegean a mile down,
the Acropolis bathed in sun where
they came with flute and sheaves. Nine
years; the temple-stairs to the sun,
the sea windswept, the same.

I think of the ninth hour, time
not to be redeemed, that lost
hour His last . . . . Saint Paul's cove
down there puts the fact
in mind; where the curve is green, the sheltering
rock below the shallower water
green, that hard man stepped . . .
But blue, blue the Aegean . . .

                    I turn to
Helios and thought of her, patient
in her ribboned hat against
the shadowed sandstone pillar
elsewhere golden there, mine,
Helios, his descendent light, and her.

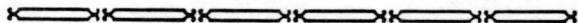

Stare into the Sun

TRIM His divinity who can, God is none of it.
There He is, absolute, helpless, being
All things, what He is, the Smiler with
The knife, Dope benevolent subscribing halos.
He's ecstasy, interstellar cold.
Men tread and plunge to fathoms. The crust's
Uncertain, he's shaken; bewildered, in his arms
Holds love squandered by indifference.
Subsequence, unpredestined, stumbles
And preparation's a waste. Buddha sits
With thumbs together, the golden phoenix crows.
Man's taken to self-abuse the world's so dull.
Exalted the priest condemns, the pincers close,
Divinity defies the mind and consequence
Is shambles. Thus

                Pentheus shears the loggy
Curls of Dionysus: He is not God.

Blaspheme who will. God is all things.
Irreproachable, shattered grace, our hatred's
His, He blazes in the impoverished stars.

Flowers at Persepolis

WE PICKED wild poppies, scarlet vivid as
Dream knows of, slender pale green
The stem, a crowd of stamens, black,
Within. Nearby, the purple thistle;
In front, hollyhocks, a row.
Magnolia was opening as sweet
On the evening air as anything in sleep.
And pansies, the scorned flower,
As simple here as any in Canada. Roses.
Roses everywhere; done with, and the white
Just coming, the red too in broken bud.
        Flowers. One holds back,
When was a list as passionate as a single bloom?
Yet here they stood where emperors had
Throne, Darius sat in ceremony,
Forty perfumed princes bearing gifts.
        One makes lists, history unaccommodated,
Of these flowers she loves.

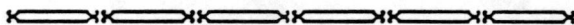

The Swans of Vadstena

ALONE she feeds the white swans.
And could I know
Her thoughts were not Leda
Enfolded in that thrashing white?

My love encloses her in a strength
Of singing white and the gold beak
Of my violence holds her.
How should she not know?

Where I stand apart, she leans
On the grass by the white swans
As they come to her on the surface
Of the water. Where they move perfectly,

She turns from the violence
To my violence, taken in the white
Tumult, unbelieving, making known
And whole the blemished god.

Landscape with Salmon Roses

FOR NO REASON the salmon-rose
Splashed colour, even the air
Capable as always in the lungs,
Had brush-strokes of it full of sun.

Oh this was a day, all right, morning
And evening in it, joy between;
Joy, meaning grief too, of course,
Death making the haystooks leap

As the roses on her table leaped
Glorious—the fields tied into
Rectangles ready for local carts,
Half-happiness at least, at home.

The ordinary was about the only reason
For the sun to smash water, the air
To have morning light in it, the roses
To exact equality with grief.

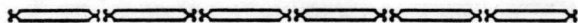

Gold Bird, Green Boxes

I LOOKED OUT the same window
And petals scattered the grass
(*Where snow had lain*).

At the next window, I discovered,
Where the road is, white
Petals all over.

We were surrounded. Nothing mattered.
A yellow bird moved at the foot of
The cedars, the hedge.

Nothing could stop the brilliance, the going
From colour to colour, from furled bud
To breaking.

The winter stream by the apple tree
Was gone. Petals were everywhere,
An ambush of them . . .

I heard the stair, her going
Downstairs to paint
Window boxes

Green, first the liquid coating
To make them impervious to the rain,
Then the permanent

Green. The whole consideration,
The window-box that would be green,
Discarded petals,

The bird, I should have known about.
There was too much to know all at once,
Entanglements,

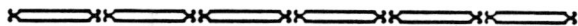

But with care the combined strengths,
The inextricable advancements,
Could be separated.

The First Faint Stars Were Out

THE FIRST FAINT STARS were out,
Jupiter was up and
Following-Saturn,
And all the curve of heaven
Blue. Dragged constellations were certain,
Beauty was possible:
An hour's magnificence,
Then night across the bay.

Each and each,
Waves broke
Endlessly. Brevity
Was certified.
Driving up that beach
To the rock where she was,
Undertides
Broke.

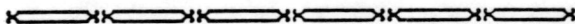

All the Night on Love Depended

THE MOON was up, half of it, vague,
White, it could pull no tide,
The last six birds flew south. A red
Boat rocked, the lake never
Still. Lights were come on,
Evening darkening the road, the cars
Driving home, the age without
Grace, itself its own criterion.
O all the night on love depended.
The lights came on, the valley darkening,
In the half light the high birds seeking
The south, cars passing along
The road by the lake never still.

Final Snow Falls and Branches

FINAL SNOW falls and branches
Wait. The mantel above the hearth
Where blossoms of forsythia are placed is bare.
I listen to Liszt's *Funérailles*,
The world white and that swift passage
Not only to spring, learned.
My heart turns to her, turns
From elegy. Beautiful the music, the snow
Falling, the inescapable hour.

Of Cordwood and Carmen

STACKING WOOD to broadcast *Carmen*.
Dumped in the driveway four runs
Of birch to keep in front of the fireplace
Warmth, and her in the basement
Piling the future, gloves and purple tuque
And topboots on, disposition as ever
Not a hurt
Towards anyone's life. Arranging wood,
She hums offkey with Bizet,
Love and that spade, the ace of Death.
Death, what hope for you!
Up through the floor I listen
To clunking cutwood birch stained with snow.
Outside, a copper sun; branches black
Against the coming snow. Day
Sets and not many to count.
She hums.

My Love Eats an Apple

SHE BITES into the red skin
Of the white hard apple in bed
And there is joy in heaven
Like innocence and whitefalls
Of snow and waters dancing up
In among green trees perched with more
Apples in tight skin
Hard as a bite and containing
Seven-eighths applesap deadpan.
I try to distil this knowledgeable joy
In crunching heaven.
God sits up there amongst
His shamefully nude nudgers,
Praising sin,
The juice of the plucked
Happy apple
In great psalms and paeans
Dripping down His testamentary beard.

Hunter's Moon

THE MOON WAS GOLD and the leaves were gold.
The red leaves had fallen and the pallor
Of the soft aspen was lighted, as gold,
By the hunter's moon, the first full
Moon of October. She stood on the verandah,
Facing that upper gold moon
(*My arms lightly, closely around her*
As if the time would come now).
Foliage was fallen thickly, the lawn
Almost uncertain, the dry brown leaves
Fallen. Across the pathway
The last flowers, a further frost
Was promised.

         She did not like the deer
To be in the forested hills. It is a hunter's
Moon, she said. But it was beautiful,
The dense covered hills, the moon above,
The moment, the way it was,
The moment.

VIII   Poems on Themselves and Music

To Give Intuition a Certitude

1

THAT is the thing: that the Light
May become crystal; that the root
Earth-covered, dusted with mud
Trampled by centaurs, hoof in soil,
That the root be yellow blossoms, petals;
That she may touch you, fragile as flake
And as cool, the desire known without reason,
The logic not known, who takes syllogism
To love? the need made immediate.

2

That faith be visible: the hoist and tackle
Of workmen, multifoliate stone;
Great pillars, vaulted, ambulatory,
In the dark, windows set between,
Crimson between, blue and ochre,
Seasoned, pitted at back by rain,
Colour shattered thus, light
Whereby men walk at Chartres
If not with Christ then that gravity
Drawing men from continents—stains,
Windows, sermons without cantation,
Green, and brown, Solomon's face
Brown as autumn leaves, with wisdom,
The durance of things, held in tracery,
Pliable lead heavy with the moulding to
Exactness by the vitraillists,
Designs of guildsmen, crimson set
And phosphor colours burnt in glass,
Brazier fires in the echoing corridors,
Green set, and brown, books
Without grammar and hornlight: a cathedral.

3

So, poem segregates
Principle; granite is thus charged,
Inflexion through point and mallet
Seared with the core of the flame;
Is music structured in the mind:
Compulsions, as oceans move on shore-lines;
Thus the lover distils by movement
The hidden charges of the heart.

4

No man endures by reason
Alone and thought—foolishness that need not
Be said.

5

So Donatello cast
Clay; Angelico kneeling moved his
Brush; on his back there,
Michelangelo believing
He did more than paint; Beethoven
Not hearing, always on the move,
No landlord in Vienna wanting
More than a year of chamber pots;
Saint Thomas watering his roses.
So the least with pot and word
And brush make palpable what he goes on:
The intuition of his love.

Thus have we altercations, sorts,
Illogicals that this love be made
Imminent.

6

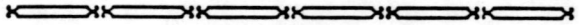

That the desire
Be without reason; that the logic be love.

The Dancing Bones

Too eminently sane!
Those mad had it: the vain
Dishabiliment, the rage, in the hard grass
The hare trembling, the wild
Paroxysm of the broken bud, the child
Behind the sofa stricken crying. Off
Off, all lendings! O, this love
Shakes me too!
Be true, be true!
Yet, yet
The rage is to be observed,
Wildly moved
Is less; with the cool thought,
Had. I call up mirrors, hot
With the dying dance,
To make the despaired poor thrust, with that glance,
Eminently mad. More mad
With that discipline made!
Intellect drums the dancing bones.
Madness dances in the bare demesnes.

The Setting Aside of Words

Music, whose thought is sensation,
Whose sensation is structure.

. . . a crafted silence shifts the heart.

No worker of music wrote poems.

Than Ancient Temples

What sweet sounds, sweet water-sounds,
Heard in Bali. O the gods are pleased,
The ancestral, gentle gods! Two small
Mallets each for his ten metallic keys,
The *gangsa*, cross-legged the four play:
The left for song, the right, as temples, far
Distant, attendant of the gods, dancers,
Ten, attendant in devotion; silken
Waters, delicate O so delicate sounds
Than ancient temples, wind-touched crystal,
White birds; a welcome music, without
Name, not for use, not for use!
A homage, the gong; each telling told again.

Listening, the four play. What matter—we,
Debussy—of us what matter who hears it?
The sweetness is of itself, its structure
Adoration, more adoration than girls,
With flowers, at temples; than silence listening heard.

Twelfth-Century Music

WHERE THE CATHEDRAL yard holds regals,
Tambourine shivers and shawms take cold.
The mason puts his tools away,
His truth-telling chisel and his gospel
Square; listens. The carpenter climbs
Down his ladder and the glazier from
His crosshatch scaffold; his head shakes
At what the carver has done, the abbot
Crosseyed with his tongue raspberried
On a corbel. They hark to the rebec and the drum
Beating out contagious measure.

O the great joy as the house
Of the Virgin is blessèd built up!
The noise and O the nooks and niches
Of the saints standing near the elegies
Of glazed glass leaded in!
What praying and incompletion!

                            The far
Fields stretch away to the linns.

Around and around, girl and boy
Bow and dance to the nasaling music.
The prebendary looks on stingily.

What warmth to the soul! Clotilde is shy.
O the Round of the Incarnation!

Couperin-le-Grand in Turkey

—after finding records by
Wanda Landowska in Istanbul

Birds, sweet birds.
Why birds?
        Why,
those turns and graces,
gruppetti, shakes
and trills and you,
Wanda, at the sweet
harpsichord.
Branches are green,
spring-green branches
and birds among.
But wait . . . . This
is sad, the mordent's
mordant, minor,
for all the crafty
shifts and contiguous
turns. Who ever
heard a sad
bird? a minor
thrush and dirgeful
dove, one
with diminished seventh?
I suppose this day
is over. For brave
modes only,
François wore
his major wig.

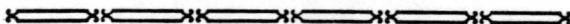

Franz Liszt: Tivoli

FOUNTAINS,
A thousand fountains
In amongst trees,
The black cypresses.
Here at Villa d'Este
The old man walked,
Honey in his tea,
Writing to princesses,
His feet
In the carpet slippers—
Composing the future.
Birds threaded the sound of water.
"Wie *lang?*"
How long?
His music unheard
Who refused to jump through Europe's hoop.
The sound of waters remembers
An old man,
The black cypresses cast shadows
Among the waters.

Six Preludes

Prelude 1 *(Appalachian)*

NORTH BOY,
Toes round wharf-edge
Nimble on foot-pads
Poised there, what mischievous
Music pommels
Your pointed ears?

What pool-plucked oboe
Bids you, slight
In generous June,
Dangerously listen
Above blue water?

(Would Pan peer
From lake-bushes,
Ivory pipe
Stained with chewed
Chokecherry?)

Heeding, wide-eyed,
Pert woodwind,
What are you about,
False faun puzzled
There, phallus
Slant in the
Caprid curls?

Hoy! wrong reckoner—
   Leap!
      Split blue!

Prelude 2 (after Picasso)

Cheeks bulged,
Slant eyes thwart
The staggering straw
Sweet still with the wet of water
Where one
Hoof bubbles the tilted stream,
Bothered by crocus
And munched acorns,
Instant ears
To the swarded thunder of centaurs
Incurious,
Flutes Pan
His nutmeg notes.

    six floors off the Avenue
    the *vernissage* conjures a marvel
    of dentine and mink

Prelude 3 (after a Tournai tapestry)

Hard excuse they had
Amid the flower-pelted almond wood
To slay the snowy unicorn.
In chamlyt slashed and gardid ciclatoun
For very courtesy yclad,
By silver bits
Their creamy stallions
Crimson-tipped for frantic love
The huntsmen hold
Haughty
Whiles from gentle beast
Against the royal
Failure
Five mutes filch
The rippled horn

Prelude 4 (after Debussy, Place Jeu de l'Arc, Geneva)

Afternoons
The leaves spill molten sun
Too hot to hold;
At the public fountain, fills,
Quenched with the white slow snows
Of mountains,
A green bottle:
Through the heard coolness
Hauling his happened *grandpère,*
The small boy licks his chocolate world.

Prelude 5 (after Ravel)

Mermaid,
She stretches . . .
The tips of the tilt of
Her breasts
Little coral.
Weary
Of caverns and bubbleless blue
She longed for seaspray.
On the rock of the reef,
Ocean
Its best
Torn turquoise
And shatter of gold,
She yawns.
   Excusably:
      In mariners' measure,
      The extent of the scale of her tail
      Not higher,
      Of course.

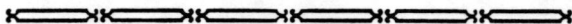

Prelude 6 (Dionysian)

Milk-white
Of ecstasy
Leans the
Drenched hyacinth

At the stable,
Hitched by a groom in mortal,
The Grecian nag
Off courtyard cobbles
With slender forehoof
Strikes
Imperious rubies.

IX Coda

Serenade for Eight Winds

AND SO I greet the spring, not as one
Given yet a greatness of flowers: but lateness!
The hyacinth has streaks of memorable rust,
Noise of sworded grating in its leaves.
Sun clashes memory. A struggle I'd
Bequeath to birds and so have done with it.
I would appear, be tall as my shadow on
This grass; morning is a beginning, not
A mourning of heavenly doves. Meridians weigh me
Down. There spring stops.

Beyond that conquest there is summer come,
Not reminiscences. The ancient mind
Runs backward needlessly. The April crocus
Has no need of memory; one planted bulbs
Last autumn to have their snowy resurrections
For themselves. Cancellation is soon
Enough without the help of pedagogy
Learned before. Hard to learn is this.
Pain reminds us of a former sleep
And fifty seasons are a fear.

. . . A student knocks at the door, come to learn of
Transient books . . . Sundials interrupt
The smell of lilac on the air. I give in.
Relinquishment of every spring so near,
I vote abstractions paramount, put out
The burning of the rose, brevities at
My mouth, under my hands the page predicted
Not yet come-to is a stumbling music whose present
Is very pulse and ear. I am committed,
Fifty seasons not enough.

O I'd submit, protest, submit again,
Music, poem bungled; defend it all!
Nothing short of preposterous will do:
Fifty more on fifty guaranteed,
I have no memory of the hyacinth's rust,
Cognizance of winter is but a matter
For asides, perfection occupies
The mind, ironies the right way round:
How the articulate flesh is first of all
And time without priority.

BLACK SWAN BOOKS
Literary Series

- ☐ H. D., *Bid Me to Live*
- ☐ H. D., *Hedylus*
- ☐ LAWRENCE DURRELL, *The Ikons*
- ☐ D. H. LAWRENCE, *Ten Paintings*
- ☐ ADRIAN STOKES, *Unity of the Stream*
- ☐ VERNON WATKINS, *With All the Views*
- ☐ W. B. YEATS, *Byzantium* (ill.)
- ☐ MICHAEL HAMBURGER, *Variations*
- ☐ PETER WHIGHAM, *Things Common, Properly*
- ☐ PETER RUSSELL, *All for the Wolves*
- ☐ PETER JONES, *The Garden End*
- ☐ RALPH GUSTAFSON, *At the Ocean's Verge*
- ☐ EZRA POUND / JOHN THEOBALD, *Letters*

Catalogue available